DUCK AND GOOSE COOKBOOK

A. D. Livingston

STACKPOLE
BOOKS

Published by
STACKPOLE BOOKS
5067 Ritter Road
Mechanicsburg, PA 17055

Cover illustration by Sandy Blair

Cover design by Caroline M. Stover

Printed in the United States of America

10 9 8 7 6 5 4 3 2 1

Library of Congress Cataloging-in-Publication Data

Livingston, A. D., 1932–
    Duck & goose cookbook / A. D. Livingston. — 1st ed.
      p.   cm.
    Includes index.
    ISBN 0-8117-2742-4 (alk. paper)
    1. Cookery (Ducks)   2. Cookery (Game)   I. Title.
TX750.5.D82L58   1997
641.6'91—dc21   97-10729
                                                CIP

ACKNOWLEDGMENTS

The author would like to thank many friends, sportsmen, and cooks who have contributed to this book. Specific acknowledgments to cooks and duck hunters, other books, and authors are made in the text as appropriate. Also, a few of the recipes were used, in slightly altered form, in the author's regular fish and game cooking column for *Gray's Sporting Journal,* and a few other recipes were adapted from the author's *Complete Fish & Game Cookbook,* published by Stackpole Books.

Other Stackpole Books by A. D. Livingston

Venison Cookbook
Wild Turkey Cookbook
Bass Cookbook
Trout Cookbook
Saltwater Fish Cookbook
Complete Fish & Game Cookbook
Shellfish Cookbook (in preparation)

CONTENTS

Introduction   vii

ONE   Ducks and Geese in the Oven   1

TWO   Ducks and Geese in the Skillet   27

THREE   Frying Ducks and Geese   48

FOUR   Ducks and Geese in the Big Pot   55

FIVE   Steamed and Simmered Ducks and Geese   69

SIX   Grilling and Smoking Ducks and Geese   75

SEVEN   Broiled Ducks and Geese   87

EIGHT   Pies and Casseroles   92

NINE   Soups, Stews, and Gumbos   101

TEN   Giblets and Appetizers   117

ELEVEN   Marinades, Sauces, and Go-withs   130

           Appendix A:
             A Culinary Guide to Ducks and Geese   150

           Appendix B:
             Ten Steps to Better Ducks and Geese   156

           Appendix C:
             Metric Conversion Tables   162

           Index   164

INTRODUCTION

Duck hunters stand divided. The culinary purist, rather rare these days, I suspect, will want the bird cooked very quickly in a hot oven, nicely browning the outside while leaving the inside meat red and moist. More squeamish sports will want the inside meat moist and pink, or medium rare, but they don't want a pool of blood on the plate. I suspect that the majority of my readers will fall into the second category, as I do. If you are serving mixed company, there is a way that may satisfy both types. As soon as the cooking timer sounds off, turn off the oven heat. Take out the birds to be served rare and put them on a heated platter. Let the other birds coast a few minutes in the hot oven.

Apart from the two camps described above, other people will want their duck well done, in which case roasting is definitely not the way to go. Dry duck or goose is simply not good in either flavor or texture. For these people, steamed duck, stews, and soups are the way to go, as discussed in the various chapters.

In any case, I trust that the recipes in the following chapters will whet most appetites and will contain something for every palate.

Appendix A contains some basic information on the culinary merits of the various species of ducks and geese, and appendix B sets forth ten steps toward putting better duck and goose on the table. Never forget that the essential steps to good wildfowl and game cookery start with the hunter.

—A. D. Livingston

ONE

Ducks and Geese in the Oven

Although the term "roast duck" has a good, time-honored, and useful connotation for a book like this and conjures up an image of a crisply brown, tasty bird, I decided not to use the word *roasted* in the chapter heading. Why? Because it means different things to different cooks and even to people who write cookbooks and culinary articles. James Beard, for example, spoke of roasting ducks over charcoal, but I hold this to be grilling. In my book, a roasted duck is cooked uncovered in the oven. But remember that ducks can also be cooked in the oven by other methods. When you seal a bird inside a "roasting bag," for example, it isn't really purely roasted. It's partly steamed. Yet, it seems to me that both methods fit nicely into this chapter. Maybe I worry too much about semantics, whereas it's the results on the table that really matter. So, let's get on with it.

Rare Roast Duck

Pluck and draw the duck. Preheat the oven to 550 degrees. Salt and pepper the duck inside and out, then roast it uncovered in the center of the oven for 12 to 20 minutes, depending on the size of the bird and how rare you want the meat. Try teal and small ducks for 14 minutes; mallards and large ducks, 18 minutes; those in between, 16 minutes. (Putting several birds into the oven will increase the ideal cooking times.) Do not baste or open the oven while cooking. Serve hot.

See also Duck Barsness later in this chapter.

1

Pseudonym Medium-Rare Duck

I found this recipe in *Game Cookery,* by E. N. and Edith Sturdivant, who said it was contributed by Francis H. Ames, author of several outdoor books, who in turn got it from Ted Trueblood, the noted and statistically suspect *Field & Stream* writer.

> 1 mallard-size duck per serving
> chopped apple
> chopped celery
> chopped onion
> salt and pepper

Pluck the birds, salt and pepper inside and out, and stuff with a mixture of chopped apple, celery, and onion. Preheat the oven to 575 degrees. Place the stuffed ducks, uncovered, on a rack in a baking pan. Center the pan in the oven. Roast for 30 minutes. Serve with vegetables, rice, bread, and red wine.

Duck John Hewitt

To my way of thinking, John Hewitt, senior editor at *Gray's Sporting Journal,* turned out to be an interesting but somewhat unbibulous fellow. I can't say that he was in any way snooty about what he drank, and I'll point out that he didn't utter a harsh word as we polished off a bottle of Gallo's Livingston Cellars Burgundy, available at Bruno's, my local supermarket, at $2.99 the bottle, complete with a cork.

It was Sunday night, I might explain, when Hewitt arrived at my place. He had driven down from Atlanta in a rental car, having flown to that city from Fairbanks, Alaska, accompanied by a tall Chesapeake Bay retriever by the name of Carl. Somewhat embarrassed about the depleted condition of my bar, I tried to explain that it's illegal to sell alcoholic beverages on Sunday in this neck of the woods and that he had telephoned too late for me to stock up. Hewitt listened politely, took a sip of the Livingston Cellars vintage, and replied that no apology was necessary.

After the wine was gone, the only alcohol I had left in the house was half a bottle of ouzo. There was a dusty jug of booze out in a toolshed, hidden there by a previous owner, but it was home-brewed stuff that smelled more of vinegar than wine. So, it was ouzo or nothing. After taking a sip of it, Hewitt made a face and grabbed the bottle to read the label, which was in Greek, as if he couldn't believe it.

"My son brought it to me from Europe," I said, taking a sip. "Smells like jelly worms, don't it?" I added, referring to the anise that the Greeks put into ouzo and American lure makers put into plastic worms.

"That's the second worst alcoholic beverage I ever tasted in my entire life," Hewitt said. The very worst alcoholic beverage he had ever tasted in his entire life, he went on at some length, was some potion he once encountered in a Canadian bar. As he related the story with consummate skill and great enjoyment, I set about cooking supper.

Before Hewitt's arrival, I had caught some bass fresh from the cypress pond behind my house and therefore had the makings of a famous Livingston fish fry, in which Hewitt had previously expressed an interest. I prided myself, and still do, on the fact that the world's best fried fish recipe comprised only four ingredients: fish, cornmeal, peanut oil, and salt. Moreover, my definitive hush puppy recipe was made with only three ingredients: cornmeal, salt, and peanut oil, plus a little water for mixing. Hewitt kept an eye on the cooking, and he ate the fried bass with enthusiasm, allowing that it was indeed good. He did, however, point out that his cousin so-and-so back in Kansas fried such small fish whole and that his uncle so-and-so back in Kansas used a larger cast-iron skillet. My fried corn pone was another matter. He didn't say anything *against* the bread, you understand, but he kept nibbling on a piece, looking at it, tasting, sniffing, as if it were strange stuff. I sensed that he was a yellow-meal man, in which case I knew that we had nothing to discuss concerning this matter. Carl, however, gulped down a pone and whined for more, as if he had finally found the true hush puppy here in the Deep South. He was a fine dog.

3

While sipping on the ouzo after dinner, I asked Hewitt for his favorite duck recipe, and he gave it to me freely. The list of ingredients was so short that the recipe went beyond itself, suggesting perhaps a short book on the subject of how to cook good fish and game with four ingredients or less.

The specifications for cooking this recipe apply only to mallard-size ducks, Hewitt said at some length, and must be followed exactly. I second the statement, as I have always maintained, and sometimes argued, that technique is far more important than a long list of ingredients. I'm also sure that most of my readers will also appreciate the culinarily spartan list in Hewitt's great recipe:

> mallard-size ducks
> heavy-duty aluminum foil

Pluck and draw the ducks. If you've got a choice, use birds that haven't been shot up too badly, saving the others for gumbo or soup. For each duck, tear off two sheets of heavy-duty aluminum foil. Place the duck breast side up on a sheet of foil, then put the other sheet on top. Bring the sheets together at the edges, squaring them up nicely, and make a fold all the way around. Then make a tight fold in the first fold, thereby sealing in the ducks. Preheat the oven to 400 degrees. Cook the duck in the center of the oven for 35 minutes. Reduce the heat to 325 and cook for 3 hours. Unwrap the birds, exposing the breast. The duck will be so tender that the meat will part and fall right off the breastbone. Have salt and a pepper mill at hand for those who want a little seasoning.

Hewitt is aware that many other gourmets insist on serving duck quite rare, and he admits that he too likes it that way. But, he says, all his kids simply love the duck cooked this way and it is very easy to eat, whereas rare duck meat doesn't fall away from the bone and may require considerable carving or gnawing at the table. It's a very good point.

Duck Barsness

Shortly after the Duck John Hewitt recipe was loosed to the world in *Gray's Sporting Journal,* John Barsness became the new editor. Fearing the worst, I wrote him for his favorite duck recipe, to which he replied, "I'm afraid my only waterfowl recipe is pretty common: I cook an unstuffed, plucked duck in a 500-degree oven, 15 minutes for a teal, 25 minutes for a mallard or other big duck, and 20 minutes for ducks in between. The point is to sear the outside and leave the inside rare. Of course, this splatters duck fat all over the oven, so it helps to either line the oven with foil or have a self-cleaner.

"Meanwhile, I'm cooking a sauce with some sort of berry jelly (chokecherry or elderberry works great, though regionally buffalo-berry is tops), red wine, minced garlic, and butter. Sauté the garlic quickly in the butter, then add jelly and wine. I don't usually measure, but I'd guess 2 garlic cloves, 1 tablespoon of butter, 3 tablespoons of jelly, and ¼ cup of wine would approximate the final result."

Duck Genghis Khan

According to George Leonard Herter, coauthor of *Bull Cook and Authentic Historical Recipes,* Genghis Khan liked Chinese food above all other. But, Herter goes on, most of what Americans call Chinese food really isn't authentic, except for the soy sauce. He says that chow mein and chop suey were invented in San Francisco by a Greek named John Metaxa. In any case, the recipe below was surely influenced by ancient Chinese cuisine. Ducks have always been popular in China, and even today they are more widely eaten than chicken in that vast country. Oranges, which are widely used in duck recipes, originated in China. The rhubarb used in the recipe is also of Chinese origin (at least, it was first mentioned in a Chinese herbal dating back to about 2700 B.C.) and was probably brought across the Asian steppes by the Mongols, who, according to Herter, believed that eating it restored a man's strength after spending the night with a woman. I wouldn't know about that, but I do know that rhubarb adds a very good flavor to wild duck.

Herter didn't specify cooking times or oven temperature for the recipe, so I have attempted to fill in the gaps myself. Also, Herter says to skin the duck. I prefer to leave the skin on, unless I have good reason to believe that it will give the duck a fishy flavor.

The Bird
1 large wild duck
lots of rhubarb, chopped
3 tablespoons cinnamon
1½ cups sugar or honey
water
salt

The Sauce
2 tablespoons butter
2 tablespoons flour
1 cup cold orange juice
1 tablespoon sugar or honey
¼ teaspoon salt

Preheat the oven to 350 degrees. Mix 2 or 3 cups of chopped rhubarb with the cinnamon and sugar or honey. Sprinkle the duck inside and out with salt, then stuff it with this mixture. Put a layer of chopped rhubarb in the bottom of a cast-iron Dutch oven or other suitable pot. Place the duck in the pot, add a cup of water, then completely cover the duck with more chopped rhubarb. Cover the pot tightly with a lid, then put it into the center of the preheated oven. Cook for 60 minutes, checking the duck from time to time and adding a little more water if needed.

As the duck cooks, melt the butter in a skillet on medium heat. Remove the skillet from the heat just as the butter starts to brown. With a wooden spoon, stir in the flour, mixing well. Stir in the cold orange juice, sugar or honey, and ¼ teaspoon salt. Mix well, then put the skillet back onto the heat. Stir until the sauce thickens.

Remove the duck from the pot and carve it into serving pieces, discarding the rhubarb. Spoon the sauce over each helping. Serve with rice, vegetables, and bread. Herter said, "This is rare delicious eating." I agree.

Roast Duck with Rum

I'm not sure, but I suspect this to be an old New England recipe. In Colonial days, rum was available from the trade with the West Indies. Beach plums and cranberries are New England products, and oranges were popular imports because they have a relatively long shelf life. In any case, be sure to try the recipe.

    4 large wild ducks
    apple chunks
    orange wedges
    soft bread crumbs
    16 ounces cranberry sauce
    1 jar beach plum jelly, 8-ounce size
    ½ cup island rum
    juice of 1 lemon
    salt and pepper

Pluck the ducks, then sprinkle them inside and out with salt and pepper. Preheat the oven to 375 degrees. Stuff the ducks with a mixture of chopped apples, orange wedges, and soft bread crumbs. Then place the birds in a greased baking pan breast side up. Mix the cranberry sauce, beach plum jelly, rum, and lemon juice. Baste the birds all over, using all of the mixture. Put the birds into the center of the oven. Bake uncovered for 60 to 80 minutes, or until the birds are medium rare, basting from time to time. Serve hot.

Clay Pot Duck

There are several clay cooking pots on the market. These utensils are somewhat oval in shape and separate lengthwise. The idea is to soak both halves of the pot in water, place the food in the bottom half, fit the halves together, and place the whole into a hot oven. The water in the clay creates steam, which in turn keeps the meat moist. Some of these clay pots are glazed, which may prevent them from soaking up and releasing much moisture. The glazed pots are, however, much easier to clean. The unglazed pots are probably better for cooking, but they are easy to crack and hard to clean. Suit yourself. In either case, the soaked pots are put into a cold oven, which is then turned on at a high heat. Putting the cold pot into a hot oven can cause rapid and uneven thermal expansion, which can easily crack the pot.

The clay pot can produce some wonderful wild ducks. (Domestic ducks are too fat and fill the pot up with grease, unless they are skinned and trimmed.) It's best to use large wild ducks, such as mallards or black ducks. Of course, if you want to cook more than one duck, you'll have to use more than one pot.

> 1 large wild duck or small goose (brant)
> 1 long carrot
> 3 or 4 green onions
> large mushrooms, sliced
> ½ cup beef broth
> ½ cup red wine vinegar
> 1 tablespoon Chinese duck sauce or tart plum jelly
> salt and pepper
> flour paste (1 tablespoon water and ½ tablespoon flour)

Soak both halves of the clay pot in cold water for 20 to 30 minutes. Dress the duck whole, rub it with wine vinegar, and sprinkle it inside and out with salt and pepper. Scrape the carrot and cut it into quarters, lengthwise. Cut the green onions in half lengthwise, including about half of the green tops. Put the carrots and onions into the bottom of the pot, then arrange a layer of sliced mushrooms on top. Place the duck, breast side up, atop the mushrooms. Mix the rest of the red wine vinegar with the beef broth, then pour it over the duck breast. Place the top part of the clay pot over the bottom part and put the unit into the center of the oven. Turn the heat to 500 degrees and cook for 1 hour. Then, using heavy gloves, carefully open the pot. Carefully remove the duck and place it onto a serving platter or plate. Arrange the carrots, onions, and mushrooms around the bird. Pour the pot juice into a saucepan. Thicken on low heat with the flour paste. Stir in the Chinese duck sauce or tart plum jelly. The wild beach plum jelly made along the New England coast is ideal. Serve the sauce with the duck, along with fluffy rice and steamed vegetables.

Wild Duck Baltimore

Here's a great duck recipe from Maryland. It's a little time-consuming, as the birds require simmering and sautéing as well as roasting. But it's worth the effort. The birds should be plucked instead of skinned.

> 2 large wild ducks, quartered
> 1 cup beef broth
> ½ cup red wine
> 1 medium onion, chopped
> 4 ounces fresh mushrooms, sliced
> 3 tablespoons butter
> 2 tablespoons flour
> 2 bay leaves
> salt and pepper
> water
> parsley (for garnish)

Place the duck quarters in a large pan and cover with lightly salted water. Bring to a boil, reduce the heat, and simmer for 20 minutes. Drain the ducks and pat dry with paper towels. Heat the butter in a skillet. Brown the duck pieces. Place the browned pieces in a greased 12×8×2 baking dish. Preheat the oven to 350 degrees.

Add the flour into the drippings in the skillet, stirring constantly with a wooden spoon. Add the beef broth, mushrooms, onion, wine, bay leaves, salt, and pepper. Simmer, stirring as you go, until the mixture is thick and bubbly. Pour the sauce over the ducks. Cover the ducks and bake in the center of the oven for 1 hour and 20 minutes. Place the birds on a serving platter. Discard the bay leaves, then pour the drippings from the baking pan over the ducks. Garnish with parsley and serve hot. Feeds 2 to 4. Personally, I'll want a whole bird.

Roast Wild Duck with Red Cabbage

The Northern Europeans are very fond of eating cabbage with duck and grease. Here's a wonderful dish that calls for red cabbage, which makes for a prettier table than ordinary cabbage.

> 2 mallard-size wild ducks
> ¼ pound salt pork
> 1 head red cabbage, cored and shredded
> 1 large onion, chopped
> ½ cup red wine
> juice of 1 lemon
> 1 teaspoon caraway seeds

Preheat the oven to 350 degrees. Dice the salt pork into ¼-inch squares. Fry the salt pork bits in a cast-iron or heavy skillet until the oil cooks out and you have some crispy, tasty cracklings. Drain the cracklings, leaving the grease in the skillet. On high heat, sear the ducks in the hot grease, browning the breast skin nicely. Place the ducks into a greased baking pan. Sauté the cabbage and onion in the skillet grease for a few minutes. Add the wine, lemon juice, and caraway seeds. Dump the skillet contents onto the ducks, spreading evenly. Bake in the center of the oven for about 1 hour, or until the ducks are done to your liking. (If uncertain, test before serving.) Serve the cracklings at the table in a bowl, to be sprinkled over servings of cabbage, baked potato, or salad. Also see Russian Goose with Red Cabbage later in this chapter.

Easy Chinese Duck

Here's a recipe that I like to cook for a special occasion. If possible, it's best to serve each partaker a whole bird. Increase the measures below if necessary. Adding more birds will also increase the overall cooking time.

> 2 mallards or other large wild ducks
> 1 cup soy sauce
> ¼ cup rice wine or vermouth
> ¼ cup brown sugar
> 6 green onions with half of tops, chopped
> 1 tablespoon grated ginger root
> 1 teaspoon five-spice powder

Pluck the ducks. Preheat the oven to 350 degrees. Grease a baking pan of suitable size. In a saucepan, heat the soy sauce, vermouth, brown sugar, green onions, grated ginger, and five-spice. Place the birds breast side down in the pan, pour the sauce over them, cover, and put into the center of the oven for 25 minutes. Increase the heat to 400 degrees, turn the birds, and bake for 15 minutes. Remove the ducks to a serving platter or plates. Stir up the pan drippings with a wooden spoon and pour them into a saucepan. Heat for a few minutes to thicken the gravy. Serve the ducks and gravy hot, along with rice and vegetables.

Twice-Baked Ducks

Here's a production that I found in *The Official Louisiana Seafood & Wild Game Cookbook*. The original called for a large can of button mushrooms, but I have changed this to 12 ounces of fresh mushrooms, which are widely available these days in our supermarkets. I have also changed "1 bunch of shallots" to 12 green onions. Like a lot of other Louisiana recipes, it tends to have lots of ingredients—but the end result is worth the trouble.

4 wild ducks
4 brandied peaches
1 large onion, finely chopped
12 green onions with half of tops, finely chopped
2 cloves garlic, sliced lengthwise into quarters
3 tablespoons chopped fresh celery leaves
12 ounces fresh mushrooms, sliced
⅔ cup spring water
½ cup burgundy
½ cup butter
6 tablespoons sifted flour
Worcestershire sauce
4 cubes beef bouillon
1 teaspoon sweet basil
⅛ teaspoon anise seeds
2 bay leaves, cut into quarters
salt and pepper

After plucking and dressing the ducks for stuffing, place them in a greased deep baking pan. Preheat the oven to 400 degrees. Salt and pepper the birds inside and out, then place a slice of garlic and a piece of bay leaf on either side of the breast of each bird. Place a little of the chopped green onion, onion, and celery tops inside and outside each bird. Put 1 tablespoon of Worcestershire sauce inside each bird, along with equal shares of anise seeds and basil. Place a brandied peach inside each duck cavity. Heat the spring water in a pan, dissolve in it the bouillon cubes, and pour over the ducks. Cover the pan and bake for 80 minutes. Remove the pan from the oven and let it stand for 30 minutes. Skim off any fat that may have risen. (Most wild ducks won't have all that much fat, though.)

While the ducks cook, melt the butter in a saucepan, add the flour, and stir with a wooden spoon until you have a brown paste. This should take 30 minutes or longer. Add the mushrooms, wine, and pan drippings. Simmer the sauce for 30 minutes, then pour it over the ducks in the pan. Cover the pan and bake for 60 minutes. Add water if needed. Serve with steamed rice, baked sweet potatoes, and the rest of the bottle of burgundy.

Russian Goose with Red Cabbage

Here's a simple but good recipe from Russia. Be sure to try it if you like cabbage as well as roast goose. A young, tender goose is best, saving the old fellows for a stew.

> 1 wild goose
> 1 head red cabbage
> 1 cup apple cider (divided)
> ¼ cup butter
> 1 tablespoon cider vinegar
> paste of cornstarch and water
> salt and pepper
> caraway seeds

Pluck, singe, and wash the goose, then sprinkle it inside and out with a little salt, pepper, and caraway seeds. Shred the cabbage, then sprinkle it with salt and pepper. In a large skillet, melt the butter. Add 2 tablespoons of the apple cider along with all the vinegar. Stir in the shredded cabbage, increase the heat, and cook for 8 minutes.

Preheat the oven to 350 degrees. Stuff the goose with the cabbage mixture. Place the goose in a roasting pan, then put it into the center of the oven. Roast until tender, basting every 15 minutes with part of the reserved apple cider and with pan drippings. In other words, use some new cider with each basting until it is used up. When the goose is done, remove it from the pan, then make some gravy by thickening the pan drippings, over heat, with a little paste made with cornstarch and water. Serve with baked potatoes.

See also Roast Wild Duck with Red Cabbage, page 10, and Roast Goose with Sauerkraut, below.

Roast Goose with Sauerkraut

Sauerkraut goes nicely with the rich meat of the wild goose, and the recipe below is one of my favorites if I've got a tender bird to work with. It's best to have "fresh" sauerkraut, but canned can be used.

> 1 young wild goose
> sauerkraut
> bacon
> bacon drippings
> salt and pepper

Pluck the goose, remove the innards, and wash the carcass inside and out. Save the giblets for making gravy for another recipe. Dry the goose, rub it with bacon drippings, then sprinkle with salt and pepper. Preheat the oven to 350 degrees. Drain the sauerkraut and stuff the bird with it. Place the bird breast side up in a baking pan and cover the breast with several strips of bacon. Put the bird into the center of the oven and bake from 15 to 20 minutes per pound, until tender. The sauerkraut helps keep the bird moist for a longer cooking time—but don't cook it *too* long. Serve the stuffing with the bird.

Rumanian Roast Duck with Corn

Here's a recipe from the Balkans, although it calls for corn, a New World gift to Europe. The ingredients list below specifies canned corn, but by all means substitute 2 cups of whole kernel fresh or frozen corn if you've got it on hand. If using frozen, let it thaw and reach room temperature before using it in the stuffing so that the cooking time will be right.

> 2 mallards or other large wild ducks
> livers from the ducks, finely chopped
> 1 can whole-kernel corn (16-ounce size)
> 3 slices bacon, chopped
> 2 slices white bread soaked in milk
> bacon drippings for baste
> salt and pepper

Preheat the oven to 325 degrees. To make a stuffing, squeeze a little of the milk out of the bread, shred it, and mix it with the corn, chopped bacon, chopped liver, salt, and pepper. Rub the duck with salt, then stuff, sew up the cavity, and place on a rack in a baking dish. Roast in the center of the oven for 1 hour, basting from time to time with pan drippings and bacon grease, or until the ducks are done to your liking.

Goose with Rice Stuffing

The stuffing and gravy from this recipe are tasty enough to save the day if the goose is no good. With a little red wine, the recipe can even save the night.

> 1 goose, dressed for stuffing
> goose giblets, diced
> 1 cup long-grain rice
> 3 cups chicken or duck broth
> ½ cup chopped white raisins
> 3 medium onions, chopped
> juice of 3 lemons
> 2 tablespoons butter
> 2 tablespoons olive oil
> 2 tablespoons chopped fresh cilantro with roots
> 1 teaspoon chopped fresh basil
> 1 teaspoon caraway seeds
> 1 teaspoon paprika
> salt and pepper

Preheat the oven to 350 degrees. Melt the butter in a skillet. Add the olive oil and sauté the onions for 5 minutes. Stir in the rice and giblets, then add 1 cup of the chicken broth. Bring to a boil, reduce heat, and simmer until the rice is almost done but not quite, about 12 minutes. Mix in the cilantro, basil, raisins, caraway seeds, salt, and pepper. Rub the goose inside and out with the juice of 1 lemon, then stuff it with the rice mixture. Pour 1 cup of the chicken broth over and into the rice stuffing. Close the opening with skewers. Sprinkle with paprika, salt, and pepper. Weigh the stuffed bird, then place it breast up on a rack in a roasting pan. Pour in the rest of the lemon juice and chicken broth. Roast for 20 minutes per pound, basting often but quickly with the pan drippings.

Picayune Canvasbacks

Many of the modern Creole and Cajun recipes have a list of ingredients as long as your leg. This may not have always been the case. The second edition of *Picayune Creole Cook Book,* published in 1901 by the *Picayune* daily newspaper in New Orleans, contains hundreds of recipes with less than ten ingredients, and, I suspect, the recipes in the first edition were even more sparse. In any case, the following recipe, quoted in full, has only two main ingredients plus a little salt and pepper and garnish. Here's the recipe, along with with a note on the ducks:

"Epicureans declare that the canvasback duck is the King of Birds, and as it feeds mostly on wild celery, it requires no flavors or spices to make it perfect. The bird partakes of the flavor of the celery on which it feeds. This delicious flavor is best preserved when the duck is roasted quickly with a hot fire [i.e., hot oven]. And so also with the dainty mallard or French ducks.

> 1 pair of wild ducks
> 1 tablespoon butter
> salt and pepper
> parsley or water cress (garnish)
> water

"Clean the ducks as you would a chicken, without scalding, however. Rinse out the inside and wipe well inside and out with a wet towel. But do not wash the duck unless you have broken the gall bladder, as the washing destroys their flavor. Rub the inside well with salt and pepper, and rub outside as thoroughly. Place a 3-inch lump of butter on the inside. Truss nicely and place the ducks in a baking pan, and brush the tops with melted butter. Pour over 2 tablespoons of water, and set in a very hot oven, and allow them to bake 20 minutes, if they are not very large, and 30 minutes, if larger than the ordinary size of canvasback ducks. A wild duck is never cooked dry. It must just reach the point where the blood will not run if the flesh is pierced with a fork in carving. When done, place the ducks in a very hot dish, and serve with their own gravy poured over them. Garnish nicely with parsley or water cress. Serve with currant jelly. Always have the plates very hot in which you serve the ducks at table."

Honey Duck

Here's an interesting dish, used also in my *Complete Fish & Game Cookbook*, that I have adapted from Sam Goolsby's *The Great Southern Wild Game Cookbook*. Use wild honey for this recipe, and inform your guests accordingly. If you don't have wild honey, lie about it.

> 2 large wild ducks
> 2 cups wild honey
> ½ cup butter
> 2 oranges (unpeeled)
> 6 tablespoons orange juice
> 2 teaspoons orange zest
> 4 teaspoons lemon juice
> 4 teaspoons salt
> 2 teaspoons ground basil
> 2 teaspoons ground ginger
> 1 teaspoon black pepper
> ¼ teaspoon dry mustard
> paste of cornstarch and water

Preheat the oven to 350 degrees. Pluck and draw the ducks for stuffing. Cut the unpeeled oranges into ½-inch slices. Mix the salt, basil, ginger, and pepper. Rub half of this mixture inside the ducks. Set the other half aside. Heat the butter in a saucepan, then stir in the honey, mustard, orange juice, lemon juice, and orange zest. Rub 2 tablespoons of this mixture inside each duck; set the rest aside. Stuff the ducks with the orange slices, then pour 2 more tablespoons of the honey mixture inside each duck. Truss the ducks. Rub the rest of the salt mixture onto the outside of the ducks.

Place the ducks on a rack in a roasting pan, pour the rest of the honey mixture over them, cover, and bake in the center of the oven for 2 hours. Uncover, baste, and bake for about 20 minutes, or until the birds are nicely browned. Place the birds onto a heated serving platter. Thicken the pan liquid with a small amount of paste made of cornstarch and water, then pour the gravy over the ducks. Serve hot.

Old Duck Bradford Angier

Here's a useful recipe from *Gourmet Cooking for Free*, by Bradford Angier, published by Stackpole Books.

"A lot of hunters like their wild ducks best roasted. You can still satisfy this preference when the bird is old and tough. Part of the secret? First simmer it slowly in salted water, with a handful of celery leaves added, until tender.

"This removes so much of the flavor that some find objectionable that you may then care to stuff the fowl. If so, for each bird sauté ½ cup of diced onion in 2 tablespoons of butter until soft but not brown. Mix this with some cooked brown or wild rice well seasoned with salt and freshly ground black pepper, an equal bulk of diced raw apple, and a scattering of seedless raisins that have been soaked in a little water for ½ hour. Sew or skewer this dressing in place.

"Rub the duck well with paprika and salt, crisscross liberally with bacon, pour a cup of good red wine over everything, and roast in a moderate 325 [degree] oven until browned, basting frequently. It will then be ready to fall apart at the touch of a fork."

Native American Stuffed Goose

Here's an adaption of a recipe that I ran across in *Native Harvests*, by Barrie Kavasch. The ingredients call for 1 teaspoon of leaves from the spicebush. This is a native American plant that was widely used by the Indians and early settlers, but usually it's the berries that are used. The recipe also calls for dill, which I doubt was a native American ingredient. Furthermore, it calls for 1 tablespoon of dill, which is enough, I think, to overpower the spicebush. Moreover, I don't think that dill and cranberries go together too nicely, but, I'll have to admit, my Indian lineage (25 percent) goes back to the Cherokee, not to the northern tribes that would have cranberries in great plenty. Anyhow, I have omitted the dill. Add some if you are so inclined.

The Bird & Gravy
1 wild goose
2 cups apple cider
paste of cornstarch and water

The Stuffing
goose giblets
2 cups cranberries, chopped
2 cups fine white cornmeal
4 ounces chopped fresh mushrooms
1 tablespoon honey
1 teaspoon chopped fresh spicebush leaves
water

Simmer the goose giblets in boiling water for 40 minutes. Drain and chop. Measure out 1½ cups of the broth, return it to the pot, and add the chopped giblets. (If you don't have 1½ cups of broth, add some water.) Thoroughly mix in the rest of the stuffing ingredients.

Preheat the oven to 350 degrees. Stuff and truss the goose, place it breast side up in a roasting pan, and roast it uncovered in the oven for 4½ hours, basting from time to time with apple cider and pan drippings.

Remove the goose, placing it onto a serving platter. Scrape the pan with a wooden spatula, mixing the pan dredgings with the drippings. Place the pan over a stove burner, tilting it a little to one end to concentrate the liquid. Slowly add a little paste made with cornstarch and water, heating and stirring until you have a smooth gravy. Serve the goose hot, along with the gravy, wild rice, stuffing, and good American vegetables such as beans, corn, and Jerusalem artichokes.

Old New England Roast Wild Duck

Here's an excellent recipe quoted from *Old-Time New England Cookbook,* by Duncan MacDonald and Robb Sagenorph.

"Singe, clean, and draw the duck. Stuff with sliced apple, chopped celery, a small amount of raw potato. Freeze overnight. Discard the stuffing. Have duck at room temperature. Dry thoroughly inside and out. Rub inside with salt. Fill cavity loosely with peeled and chopped apples and raisins. Brush with butter and place in uncovered roasting pan in moderate oven (325 degrees). For rare duck, roast 10 to 12 minutes to the pound; 15–20 minutes, well done. Baste frequently with fat in the pan, to which you may add red wine. Serve with cranberries or orange slices."

Coot Armagnac

I have adapted this recipe from *Wild Game Cookbook,* by John A. Smith, who said that it will change the name of coot from mud hen to water chicken.

> 3 or 4 coot breasts
> 2 cups pitted cherries
> ¾ cup chicken stock
> ⅓ cup Rhine wine
> ¼ cup Armagnac
> 3 tablespoons butter
> 2 tablespoons honey
> ¼ teaspoon ground cinnamon
> salt and pepper

Preheat the oven to 350 degrees. Salt and pepper the coot breasts, then roast for 30 minutes. Heat the butter in a large skillet. Add the coot breasts, turning to wet all sides. Pour in the Armagnac. Flame. Add the chicken stock, wine, honey, cinnamon, salt, and pepper. Bring to a boil, add the cherries, cover, and simmer for 10 minutes. Arrange the coot breasts on a heated platter or on individual plates, top with the cherry sauce from the skillet, and serve hot. Feeds 2 to 4.

Variation: Also try this recipe with the breasts of teal or other smaller ducks.

Roast Goose in a Bag

Sealing a goose in a plastic baking bag makes the roasting process more or less foolproof because the bird is partly steamed. The big problem comes when you take the bird out of the bag only to find that it isn't done. In other words, it's hard to test for doneness when the bird is in a bag. If this should happen, cook it for a while longer without sealing it.

> 1 wild goose, about 4½ pounds dressed
> 1 cup red wine
> 1 tablespoon flour
> 1 tablespoon celery seed
> salt and pepper

Pluck, draw, wash, and drain the bird. Preheat the oven to 350 degrees. Sprinkle the bird inside and out with salt, pepper, and celery seed. Add the flour and wine to a large baking bag and shake it around to mix. Put the goose into the bag, seal with a twist-tie or cotton string, and place it on a baking tray. Make several small holes in the top of the bag with a fork or knife point. Place it in the center of the oven. Bake for 2 hours, adding another ½ hour per pound if the bird dresses out at more than 4½ pounds. When it is done, place the bird on a serving platter. Carefully pour the juice from the bag into a saucepan. If the bird was very fatty, skim the top. Heat the juice to a boil, reduce slightly, and pour over the goose for serving.

Chef Alfred's Roast Wild Goose

Here's an excellent recipe adapted from *Our Best Recipes,* published by *Southern Living* magazine, where I was once an editor. I don't know anything about Chef Alfred, however, except that his recipe is a good one. The goose should be plucked and dressed whole. Be sure to save the liver.

> 1 large wild goose (6 to 8 pounds, dressed)
> 2 pounds potatoes
> 1 medium onion, chopped
> ¼ cup water
> 1 tablespoon butter
> 2 tablespoons bacon drippings
> ½ teaspoon dry thyme (or 1 teaspoon fresh)
> ½ teaspoon sage
> flour
> salt and pepper

Pluck and draw the goose, saving and chopping the liver. Soak the goose in cold water for 1 hour. While waiting, boil the potatoes (unpeeled) in slightly salted water until done. While the potatoes are still warm, peel and mash them. Heat the butter in a skillet, then sauté the onion and goose liver for 5 or 6 minutes; add to the potatoes, along with the thyme, sage, salt, and pepper. Use quite a bit of pepper, making a hot stuffing.

Preheat the oven to 350 degrees. Spoon the stuffing into the goose, then close with skewers and cotton cord. Place the goose breast side up in an uncovered baking pan. Baste with bacon drippings. Add the water. Bake for 1½ hours, basting often with pan drippings. Dredge the goose with a little flour, then baste with pan drippings, to make a crisp brown skin. Serve hot with applesauce (chapter 11) and vegetables.

Roast Geese with Oysters

Here's a recipe for 2 young geese and lots of oysters, which can be expensive unless you gather your own. In any case, use fresh oysters, shuck them yourself, and save the juice. Pluck and draw the birds for stuffing. You'll need a roasting pan large enough to hold the geese without much space to spare, fitted with a tight lid and a rack.

The Birds
2 young geese
Juice of 1 lemon
salt and pepper
1 cup oyster liquor
2 cloves garlic, minced

The Stuffing
1 quart oysters, with liquor
2 loaves stale white bread
1 cup butter
1 cup chopped green onions with tops
1 cup chopped fresh mushrooms
1 cup chopped celery with tops
2 tablespoons chopped fresh parsley or cilantro
3 cloves garlic, skinned but left whole
red wine
salt and pepper

Melt the butter in a large skillet. Sauté the onions, mushrooms, parsley, celery, and garlic for 5 minutes. Stir in some salt and pepper. Crumble the bread into the skillet, stirring to mix well. Add enough red wine, about 1 cup, to make a moist stuffing. In a saucepan, heat the oyster liquor. Simmer the oysters, a few at a time, in the liquor until the edges curl. Mix the oysters into the bread mixture, reserving 1 cup of the liquor. It's best to use the stuffing right away instead of mixing it ahead of time.

Preheat the oven to 350 degrees. Weigh the dressed birds. Sprinkle the birds inside and out with lemon juice, salt, and pepper. Stuff the birds, close, and arrange on a greased rack in the roasting pan. To the roasting pan, add the garlic and a cup of the oyster liquor. Cook for 20 minutes per pound (combined weight), basting from time to time with the pan drippings. Increase the heat to 450 degrees, remove the cover, and roast for a few more minutes, until the birds are nicely browned on top.

Put both birds onto a large platter and serve hot, along with vegetables, green salad, hot French bread, and, of course, the stuffing.

TWO

Ducks and Geese in the Skillet

One weekend Dr. Helen N. Livingston, my good wife, brought home a car full of junk from Havana, Florida, a quaint little tobacco town that I thought had dried up years earlier. In recent times, however, it has apparently become a sort of weekend marketplace for artists, junk dealers, craftspeople, and antiquarians.

"A. D.," Dr. Livingston said, "I have found the most wonderful leather-bound cookbook for you."

"Where is it?" I asked, looking rather skeptically at several bags of high-smelling dried potpourri that she had piled onto the table along with three live citronella plants.

"Oh, I didn't buy it," she explained. "The ATM wouldn't work. The book was written by a brigadier general and had some recipes for duck and interesting dishes from all over the world. Funny thing. The old man running the bookstore closed up for lunch and was gone for almost 3 hours."

"What sort of duck recipe?" I asked, perking up considerably. I was working toward this book at the time.

"It was a recipe called Far Eastern Duck with Guava Sauce. I knew of your fondness for guava jelly——"

"Curry?" I asked, fearing the worst.

"No. I don't think so."

That did it. It was Sunday. Dr. Livingston had other obligations, so I drove over to Havana early the next morning to get the book before somebody snapped it up—but I was quite surprised to learn that the town closed up during the week. Apparently, most of the local people already had plenty of junk, needed very little art, and used potpourri sparingly. The shops were open only on Friday, Saturday, and Sunday, the signs said, except at noonday.

Since I was already in town, I located the used bookstore so that I wouldn't have to waste any time looking for the place when I came back on the weekend, at which time the sidewalks would surely be abustle with tourists and out-of-town shoppers as well as students and faculty from Florida State University. The weathered red brick buildings and streets and sidewalks did lend a certain old charm to the little town, and I could see how it had become a regional mecca for junk lovers, crafts enthusiasts, and bookworms. There was even a sidewalk café.

I arrived in Havana at 6:45 A.M. the next Saturday morning, and I was leaning against the door of the bookstore when the proprietor arrived at 9:17 with the *Tallahassee Democrat* stuck under his arm. Without offering to help me locate the book, he grunted, sat in the barber's chair behind the counter, and started reading the newspaper. Luckily the book had not been sold, and I found it within the hour: *A General's Diary of Treasured Recipes*, by Brigadier General Frank Dorn. The recipe called "Far Eastern Duck with Guava Sauce" was exactly where the index said it was, and it contained no curry. The book did indeed have a leather or leatherette cover; more importantly, the pages were sewn together and properly bound instead of being glued in like most modern books. When I paid the man in cash, he stuck the money into his pocket, poked the book into a used plastic bag from a local IGA grocery store, snorted, and said he knew that somebody would buy it.

The old Pfleuger Akron bait-casting reel, which I bought from an antique store next door, had a worn pawl and didn't work too well even after I cleaned and oiled it. The old cast-iron wash pot, in which I planned to fry a whole wild turkey, turned out to have a hairline crack in it, no doubt because of uneven heating. But I was not disappointed with General Dorn's book, and the duck recipe proved to be a good one that can be prepared in an ordinary American skillet.

Other recipes follow, and I hope it will become apparent that the skillet is one of my favorite ways to cook. It's a hands-on process—better, in this regard, than sticking stuff into an oven. See also the skillet-frying recipes in the next chapter.

The General's Guava Duck

Although I have presumed to change the format a little and have rewritten the directions in my own words, the recipe is still essentially General Dorn's. I have, however, adjusted it for cooking 2 mallard size wild birds instead of a fat Peking duckling. You'll need a large skillet with a cover to cook the dish. Most electric skillets will do.

> 2 mallards
> flour
> ¼ cup butter
> 1 large onion, peeled and finely sliced
> 1 cup chicken stock (or water with bouillon cube)
> 4 tablespoons guava jelly
> 3 tablespoons chopped almonds
> 2 tablespoons raisins
> juice of 1 lime or lemon
> 1 clove garlic, crushed
> 1 teaspoon grated fresh ginger root
> ¼ teaspoon mace
> 6 peppercorns
> 6 cloves
> salt to taste

Pluck the ducks, quarter them, and dust the pieces with flour. Melt the butter in the skillet and brown the duck pieces on both sides. Add the onion slices, garlic, grated ginger, peppercorns, cloves, and salt. Mix together the lime juice, chicken stock, and mace; add the mixture to the skillet, along with the almonds and raisins. Stir to blend the ingredients, then cover the skillet, adjust the heat to very low, and simmer for 1½ to 2 hours, or until the duck is very tender. Take the duck out of the skillet, placing the pieces onto a hot serving platter. Add the guava jelly to the skillet, stirring until you have a smooth sauce. Pour the sauce into a gravy boat to be placed on the table. The General says to serve the duck with rice, melba toast, and orange and onion salad. The rice is essential, but I'll take hot French bread instead of melba toast. The orange and onion salad is very good if you've got mild Vidalia or Walla Walla onions at hand. I highly recommend it, made as follows:

Orange and Onion Salad
skinned orange sections
mild onions
romaine lettuce

Section the oranges and peel away the skin. This is easier if you have large navel oranges. (As it happened, on the way back from Havana I bought 2 bags of navel oranges and 10 pounds of Vidalia onions at a fruit stand at Quincy, Florida, where one of my distant relatives, Cousin Pascal, as Daddy called him, used to run a jewelry store and raise prize beagles.) Quarter the onion and separate the pieces into boats. Arrange the orange sections and onions on a slice or two of romaine lettuce. It's best to prepare each serving separately on a salad plate. Note that the General said to use chopped onions instead of slices. Suit yourself. I might add that the Turks make a similar orange and onion salad, adding olives, lemon juice, and olive oil, along with a little paprika and ground cumin seeds.

A. D.'s Electric Skillet Duck

Here's an easy recipe that I like to cook in an electric skillet. Ducks of any size will work, but I normally use only the breasts, saving the legs and frames for gumbo or some other purpose. The thighs can also be boned and cooked along with the breasts. For mallard-size ducks, allow 1 breast (2 fillets) per person. A big eater will require more, so if you are short of ducks have plenty of rice to eat with the gravy.

> 4 mallards or 8 teal, filleted
> 1 can condensed cream of mushroom soup
> (10¾-ounce size)
> 1 can condensed cream of celery soup (10¾-ounce size)
> milk
> 2 ounces cognac
> 1 ounce curaçao
> flour
> cooking oil
> salt and pepper

Marinate the duck breasts in milk for several hours. Drain, sprinkle with salt and pepper, then dust lightly with flour. Heat a little oil in the skillet and brown the duck breasts. Remove the duck breasts, setting them aside to drain. Pour most of the oil out of the skillet, then stir in the soups and curaçao. Take a sip of the cognac, then stir the rest of it into the skillet along with the duck breasts. Turn the heat to very low, cover, and simmer for 1 hour, or until the ducks are quite tender. You may have to add a little water if extended cooking time is required. Put the duck breasts on a platter and top with the gravy. The gravy can also be served over rice, or it can be sopped with Parker House rolls.

Faisinjan

This old Persian dish, calling for ground walnuts and pomegranate juice, is easy to prepare in a large skillet with a cover. Pomegranates are sold in the fall of the year, and the juice is merely squeezed from the seeds. (Be warned that the juice will stain your clothing.) If you can't get pomegranate juice, substitute the juice of 2 lemons or limes. Also, in a pinch, 2 cups of water and 2 bouillon cubes can be substituted for the chicken stock.

> 2 large wild ducks (or 4 or 5 teal)
> 2 cups chicken broth or stock
> 1 cup ground walnuts
> ½ cup pomegranate juice
> 1 medium onion, grated
> ½ teaspoon cinnamon
> butter
> salt and pepper
> rice (cooked separately)

Cut the duck into quarters. Sprinkle the pieces with salt and pepper. Heat ½ cup of butter in the skillet and cook the duck until it is almost done, turning to brown both sides. While cooking the duck, melt 1 tablespoon of butter in a saucepan and sauté the onions for 5 minutes. Stir in the ground walnuts. Add the pomegranate juice, chicken stock, and cinnamon. Cook and stir until the sauce thickens. Pour the sauce over the duck, increase the heat until the sauce bubbles, cover, decrease the heat, and simmer for ½ hour.

Variations: Some people like to add a little sugar (about 1 teaspoon) along with the cinnamon. Others will stir in 2 tablespoons of tomato paste while sautéing the onions.

Duck of '94

Living in the last house on a dead-end dirt road has its advantages and disadvantages. Accentuating the negative side, the flood of '94, as it is called in this part of the country, dumped 30 inches of water on us and washed out the dirt road. We couldn't get out by car. Our food supply was low. On the fourth day, we were down to two mallards in the freezer, a kiwifruit in the refrigerator (we still had electrical power), a bag of large Texas onions, a can or two of tomatoes in the cupboard, and such dry staples as rice—along with a yard full of pears. Our several trees were so full of fruit in '94 that the limbs were bending and breaking. The winds from the tropical storm had blown many of the pears to the ground. We had plenty of fish in the pond, but the water was high and very muddy.

Putting all this together wasn't an easy task, and I wouldn't have made the combination if I hadn't been pleasantly surprised by the orange and onion salad as served with The General's Guava Duck, above. Why not onions and pears with stir-fried duck and rice? Was the duck too tough for stir-frying? The kiwifruit, I knew, contained a natural tenderizer, so I decided to mash it up (it was already too soft to stir-fry) and marinate the ducks with it. First I filleted out the breast and boned the thighs, cutting the meat into strips for stir-frying. I saved the legs, neck, giblets, and frame for cooking another meal.

> breast and thighs from 2 large wild ducks
> 2 or 3 pears, peeled, cored, and diced
> 1 medium-to-large white onion,
>   sliced lengthwise into boats
> 1 kiwifruit
> 1 tablespoon soy sauce
> black pepper (optional)
> rice (cooked separately)
> peanut oil
> ½ teaspoon brown sugar
> cinnamon

Put the sliced duck meat into a nonmetallic container. Peel the kiwifruit, mash it, and mix it in with the duck, along with a little black pepper, if you want it. Set aside for 2 hours.

Heat a little peanut oil in a skillet. Sauté the onion for 2 or 3 minutes. Add the duck strips, which will be coated with kiwifruit. Add any remaining kiwifruit from the bowl. At this point, your skillet will be a mess and won't resemble a stir-fry. Keep going, stirring with a wooden spoon and cooking for 5 minutes. Stir in the soy sauce. Add the pear cubes, stirring to mix, and cook for 2 or 3 minutes, stirring in the brown sugar and a little cinnamon as you go. Serve hot with rice. The duck will be tender enough to cut with a fork, and the pear cubes will retain some crunch.

The only problem with this dish is that it lacks color. The next time I cook it, I'm going to add some red and green pepper strips.

Note: Remembering the kiwifruit tenderizing trick can save the day for you when you have tough meat to cook. Kiwifruit has a long shelf life and very little waste. (The thin skin can also be placed on meat to tenderize it.) Put one or two in your bag of sugar or flour the next time you pack grub for camp.

Wild Duck with Mushrooms

Here's a skillet recipe for breast halves, legs, and thighs. Save the rest of the bird for soup. The measures below work for 1 mallard-size bird. If you use teal or other smaller birds, reduce the cooking times by about 20 percent.

> 1 large wild duck
> 8 ounces fresh mushrooms, sliced
> 1 medium onion, sliced
> 2 cups water
> ½ cup red wine
> butter or margarine (divided)
> 2 tablespoons flour
> 2 bay leaves
> ⅛ teaspoon dried thyme
> salt and pepper to taste
> rice or wild rice (cooked separately)

Pluck and draw the bird, then disjoint it, separating the leg quarters into drumsticks and thighs and splitting the breast in half. Melt 2 tablespoons of butter in a skillet and brown the duck pieces. Add the water and bay leaves, along with a little salt and pepper. Reduce the heat, cover, and simmer for 1½ hours. In a small skillet or saucepan, heat 2 tablespoons of butter. Sauté the onions for 5 minutes. Mix in the flour a little at a time on low heat, stirring as you go to avoid lumps. Mix in the mushrooms and wine, then pour the batch over the duck pieces at the end of the 1½-hour cooking period. Cover and simmer for another 30 minutes. Serve hot with rice or wild rice, steamed vegetables, and a fruit salad.

Vathoo Kari

I was surprised to learn not long ago that a genuine Indian curry doesn't necessarily contain what Americans call curry powder, thank goodness. Rather, a real curry dish is made with a blend of spices mixed together in the recipe. The fenugreek used in this recipe is a spice made from ground seeds. It is popular in India and Morocco, often used in pickles and chutneys. The recipe also calls for coconut milk. This is not the liquid inside a coconut; it is made from the meat of the coconut, as discussed in the recipe in chapter 11. If you don't want to make your own, canned coconut milk can be purchased in some shops and by mail order.

In India, this dish is cooked with a large domestic duck with the skin removed. It can also be cooked with 2 mallards or 3 (or 4) smaller wild ducks, skinned and disjointed. Since the ducks are skinned and the dish is on the spicy side, this is a good recipe to try with birds that have been eating lots of fish.

You can use a cast-iron Dutch oven, but a large skillet with a lid will also work. Either works best if it is large enough in the round to accommodate all the duck pieces at one time.

> 2 large wild ducks
> 2½ cups coconut milk (chapter 11)
> 2 tablespoons clarified butter (chapter 11)
> 1 large onion, minced
> 2 cloves garlic, minced
> 3 green chili peppers, slit lengthwise and seeded
> ¾ tablespoon finely grated fresh ginger root
> juice of 1 lemon
> 1½ teaspoons turmeric
> 1½ teaspoons ground coriander
> 1 teaspoon salt
> 1 teaspoon ground cumin seeds
> ½ to 1 teaspoon cayenne
> ¼ teaspoon ground fenugreek

Pour a little of the coconut milk into a small container and stir in the coriander, turmeric, fenugreek, cumin, and about half of the cayenne; mix this into a paste and set aside. Heat the butter in a large skillet or Dutch oven and sauté the onion, garlic, and ginger for 2 or 3 minutes, stirring as you go. Add the paste and stir for another 8 minutes, stirring in a little water if needed to keep the mixture from drying out. Add the duck pieces and sauté for 8 minutes, turning frequently. Pour in the coconut milk, then add the salt and sliced chili peppers. Bring to a quick boil, reduce the heat to very low, cover, and simmer for 30 minutes or longer, until the duck is very tender. After simmering for 15 minutes, add a little more cayenne to the sauce if needed. When the duck is done, stir in the lemon juice. Serve with lots of fluffy white rice.

Teal Jambalaya

A real jambalaya has some ham in it, for that's where the name comes from. Yet, cookbook and magazine writers have used the term so loosely that the ham is often ignored entirely, and even a gumbo is sometimes called a jambalaya. (I once helped prepare a large batch of turtle soup, made with 50 pounds of Florida softshell, and one of the cooks insisted that we call it a jambalaya!) The recipe below, I might add, was adapted from an official Louisiana work—and it called for no pork whatsoever. I have added the smoked ham hock and the smoked pork sausage. The latter should be well smoked, making it on the hard and dry side. Use venison sausage if you have it. The smoked ham hock should have quite a bit of meat on it.

The measures call for 3 teal, but 2 larger ducks can be used. You can also use a duck and 2 or 3 doves, which have similar good dark meat. In any case, cut the duck into breast halves, thighs, and drumsticks. Save the frames, necks, wings, and giblets.

Traditionally, I might add, a jambalaya is cooked in a large cast-iron skillet. It should be large enough to hold all the ingredients, and it should also have a lid. I recommend a 13-inch cast-iron skillet with a lid, but a large electric skillet will also work.

3 teal, plucked
½ pound smoked pork or venison sausage
½ pound smoked ham hock
1 quart water
2 medium onions, chopped
2 cloves garlic, chopped
1½ cups uncooked long grain rice
⅔ cup tomato sauce
½ cup cooking oil
1 rib celery, chopped (with green tops)
8 ounces sliced fresh mushrooms
¼ cup chopped green bell pepper
¼ cup chopped red bell pepper
2 tablespoons chopped fresh parsley
2 bay leaves
½ teaspoon red pepper flakes
salt and black pepper to taste

Heat the water in a pot along with the bay leaves and red pepper flakes. Add the ham hock, duck giblets, and bony pieces. Cover the pot tightly and simmer for 2 hours. Pull the meat from the bony pieces and chop the giblets. Bone the ham hock, discard the fat, and chop the lean meat. Set the chopped meats aside. Measure the broth and add enough water to yield a full quart. Discard the bay leaves.

Cut the sausage into ½-inch pieces. Heat the oil in a large jambalaya skillet, then sauté the duck pieces and sausage for 10 minutes, stirring often. Add the onions, garlic, mushrooms, and celery, then sauté for 5 minutes. Drain the oil from the skillet. Add the chopped bell peppers and parsley; cook for a few minutes on low heat, stirring. Add the broth, tomato sauce, chopped ham, chopped duck giblets, rice, salt, and black pepper. Bring to a boil, reduce the heat, cover tightly, and simmer for 20 minutes. The liquid should be absorbed by the rice, leaving a moist dish. If necessary, simmer without the lid until the liquid has been absorbed, stirring with a wooden spoon. Serve hot, along with plenty of New Orleans or sourdough French bread.

Duck with Cassis Sauce

I got this recipe from Concord Farms, which supplies ducks to the food trade. It is very good with both domestic and wild birds. Cassis is a syrup made with black currants, and I found some (made in France) at my local supermarket. The recipe calls for slightly underripe pears. I used some barnyard pears from my own trees, which are quite firm even when ripe. Soft pears will become too mushy, although the sauce will be good. Concord's recipe calls for 2 tablespoons rendered duck fat, but I usually substitute margarine when cooking wild ducks.

> breast fillets from 3 or 4 mallards, skinned
> 2 firm pears
> 2 cups dry white wine
> 2 tablespoons margarine
> 2 tablespoons sugar
> 2 tablespoons cassis
> lemon juice
> salt and freshly ground black pepper

Peel, halve, and core the pears. Put the halves into a pot or pan and cover with the wine. Add the sugar, bring to a boil, reduce heat, and simmer for 20 or 30 minutes, until the pears are tender to the fork. Set aside. Heat the margarine in a large skillet over medium heat. Sauté the duck breasts until browned on both sides. Reduce the heat and cook for a few more minutes. Remove the breasts and let them drain on a brown bag for a few minutes. While waiting, pour the fat out of the skillet and add 6 tablespoons of juice from the cooked pears. Bring to a boil and reduce by about ⅓. Add the cassis, ½ teaspoon lemon juice, salt, and pepper. Stir and taste, adding more lemon juice if needed to cut the sweetness. Slice the duck breasts diagonally and arrange overlapping slices on a warm serving platter or plate. (I prefer thin slices, especially if the wild ducks are a little tough.) Reheat the pear halves and place them on the plate with the duck slices. Pour the cassis sauce over the duck slices and serve hot.

Azerbaijani Goose

Azerbaijan, bordered by both the Caspian and Black Seas, has always been blessed with fish, game, and fowl, as well as many fruits, nuts, and fresh vegetables. This rich recipe, adapted from *Cooking from the Caucasus,* by Sonia Uvezian, calls for lots of butter—and ¾ pound of boneless goose meat per person. That's a long way from the servings that are recommended in New York cookbooks these days, and it suits me just fine, although I can make do with ½ pound of goose or duck, as it is a rich meat. The recipe also calls for rice pilaf, made from one of several recipes from the Caucasus. You can substitute ordinary steamed rice, but you really should try this recipe if you've got the time. Part of its flavor and texture comes from a crust that forms on the bottom—and that's the best part. I always start the rice pilaf first, then prepare the meat as the pilaf cooks. In any case, the pilaf should be ready before or shortly after the goose is done. The recipe calls for clarified butter, which is often used in skillet cooking because it doesn't burn easily. It's easy to make, as directed in chapter 11.

The Pilaf
1½ cups long-grain rice
8 cups water
4 tablespoons clarified butter
1½ tablespoons salt

Bring the water to a rolling boil in a large pot. Add the salt. Then add the rice slowly, so that the boiling is continuous. Boil for 10 minutes, stirring the rice several times. Drain the rice, rinse it with lukewarm water, and drain again. Heat 2 tablespoons of clarified butter in a heavy saucepan. Add a few tablespoons of the rice, mixing it with the butter and spreading it in an even layer over the bottom of the pan. Add the rest of the rice, then sprinkle 2 tablespoons of clarified butter over it evenly. Drape a towel over the pan, then put the lid on it. Bring the corners of the towel over the lid so that they won't burn on the stove.

Simmer over low heat for 30 to 40 minutes. Then spoon all the rice onto a plate or platter. If all has gone according to plan, the rice will be dry and in separate grains, and there will be a crust in the bottom of the pan. Scrape up the crust, which some people believe is the best part, and arrange alongside the white rice.

The Meat
3 pounds boneless goose meat
¼ pound dried prunes (pitted)
1 medium-to-large onion, cut in half lengthwise
    and sliced
clarified butter
½ teaspoon powdered saffron dissolved in
    2 tablespoons warm water (divided)
rice pilaf (above)
salt and pepper

Trim and skin the goose meat, cut it into 2-inch pieces, and sprinkle it with salt and pepper. In a large skillet, heat 4 tablespoons of clarified butter. Cook the goose pieces until they begin to brown on all sides, turning from time to time. Remove the goose meat, putting it on a heated plate or heated platter. Brown the onions in the skillet, stirring, for about 10 minutes. Return the goose pieces, then add the prunes and 1 tablespoon of the saffron liquid. Reduce the heat to low, cover, and simmer for 15 minutes. Add a little hot water if needed to keep the mixture moist.

When you are ready to serve, spoon 1 cup of the cooked white rice into a bowl. Mix in the rest of the saffron water, making yellow rice. Mound the remaining white rice onto a heated serving platter. Top with the goose mixture. Garnish with the yellow rice and the brown rice crust. Over all this sprinkle a little butter. Serve hot. Enjoy.

Elizabeth's Favorite Sea Duck

Outdoor columnist Steve Hickoff says that a girlfriend and game taster preferred sea duck prepared by this recipe over a greenhead cooked fast in the oven. Hence, the name. The recipe, Hickoff says, works with scoter, eider, and oldsquaw—as well as with crow breasts. Here's the recipe pretty much as Hickoff spelled it out for me:

First bleed the sea duck breasts in water—no vinegar, no salt—in the refrigerator for 4 days, changing the water with regularity until the meat goes from a burgundy to pink. On the fifth day, marinate the breasts in a mix of milk (enough to cover the breasts), Mongolian Fire Oil (just a splash or two), and crushed black pepper. Wash the breasts on day 6. Cube or finger the meat, then tenderize it with a meat mallet, beating creole seasoning into it (he sometimes cheats with Tony Chachere's). Then sauté sliced mushrooms in cheap white wine and butter, add the duck, brown, add a single splash of Mongo Oil on each cube or finger, and serve hot. Hickoff says he often serves the dish over pasta. Also try it over rice.

Hickoff also says that he sometimes omits the creole seasoning, adding instead a mix of salt, black pepper, and paprika . . . or curry powder . . . or garlic salt. Personally, I'll pass on the curry powder, but the next time I cook the recipe (and the coots that have taken up around the dock at my cabin here on Dead Lakes had better watch out), I plan to sprinkle the meat liberally with lemon-pepper seasoning before beating it.

Duck or Goose Breast Fricassee

This dish may or may not be a genuine fricassee, but it's good at home and in a duck camp.

> 4 wild duck breasts or 2 wild goose breasts
> 12 ounces fresh mushrooms, sliced
> ½ cup olive oil
> ½ cup red wine
> flour
> salt and pepper

Fillet the breasts, getting a strip of meat from either side of the breastbone. Heat the oil in a skillet, then sauté the mushrooms. With a slotted spoon, remove the mushrooms, draining them on a brown bag. Salt and pepper the duck or goose fillets, shake them in a bag with some flour, and brown them in the skillet, turning once. Pour off most of the oil from the skillet, then scrape up the dredgings with a wooden spoon. Put the duck or goose breasts and mushrooms into the skillet. Pour in the wine. Cover tightly and simmer on very low heat for 10 minutes for duck breasts or 20 minutes for goose breasts, stirring from time to time. Do not boil. Serve with wild rice, steamed vegetables, and plum sauce or Chinese duck sauce.

Sautéed Goose Breast

This recipe works with old or young goose. Skin and fillet the breast. Fillets from old birds can be pounded with a meat mallet to help tenderize the meat. You can also bone the thighs and use the meat if you don't have enough breast meat to feed everybody.

goose breast fillets
mushrooms, sliced
onions, sliced
celery, sliced
teriyaki sauce
red or white wine
flour
butter
salt and pepper

Put the breast fillets into a nonmetallic container, douse with teriyaki sauce, and marinate in the refrigerator for 5 or 6 hours. Drain the fillets, sprinkle with salt and pepper, dust with flour, and brown in butter in a skillet. Remove the duck fillets, then brown the onion. Add the celery and mushrooms; sauté for another 5 minutes. Add the browned fillets. Pour in the wine, cover, and simmer for 1 hour.

Easy Camp Duck

Here's an almost foolproof duck recipe for use in camp, if you've got a skillet or Dutch oven with a lid. Any sort of ducks can be used, but small ducks will require less vegetables. I use only the duck breasts for this recipe, saving the rest for stews and soups. For grease, I use about a tablespoon of bacon fat left over from breakfast, but any good cooking oil or butter can be used.

> 2 wild duck breasts (4 fillets)
> 1 large onion, diced
> 1 medium rib celery with tops, diced
> 1 tablespoon bacon drippings (and maybe more)
> salt and pepper
> water

Skin and trim any fat from the duck breasts, then cut them into 1-inch chunks. Heat the bacon drippings in a skillet. Lightly brown the duck meat. Remove and drain the duck pieces. Sauté the diced onion and celery for 5 minutes, adding a little more bacon drippings if needed. Put the duck pieces back into the skillet, sprinkle with salt and pepper, and pour in enough water to barely cover everything. Bring to a light boil, cover, reduce the heat, and simmer on very low heat until the meat is very tender. Stir from time to time, adding a little more water if needed. Serve the gravy with the duck, along with rice and vegetables, if available.

Skillet Duck according to Dr. Carver

The recipe below has been adapted from a recipe by a Dr. Carver of Minnesota, as published in the *Ducks Unlimited Cookbook*.

> 4 duck fillets
> flour
> cooking oil
> 1 can cream of celery soup (10¾ ounce size)
> salt and pepper

Sprinkle the fillets with salt, pepper, and flour. Beat them on both sides. Sprinkle again with flour and beat again. Repeat twice more. If you are using the edge of a plate, rotate it 90 degrees with each pounding. Heat the oil in a skillet and fry the fillets for several minutes, turning once. The oil should be quite hot, browning the outside nicely without overcooking it before the inside gets done. Drain the fillets and keep warm. Quickly pour off most of the pan grease. Scrape up any bits of flour from the bottom of the skillet and add the soup, heating and stirring as you go. Place the fillets back into the skillet and simmer for 20 to 30 minutes. Serve with rice and steamed vegetables. Use wild rice if you've got it.

Pato con Arroz

Here's a duck and rice dish that Peruvians seem to prefer to the standard Latin American *pollo con arroz* (chicken and rice). The dish can be cooked in a rather deep electric skillet or in a stove-top Dutch oven.

> 2 mallards or ducks of similar size
> 3 cups boiling water
> 1 cup rice (uncooked)
> ¼ cup butter or armadillo fat
> 1 medium onion, minced
> 2 cloves garlic, minced
> peppercorns
> coriander seeds
> cumin seeds
> sea salt

Dress and quarter the ducks. Melt the butter or fat in a skillet or stove-top Dutch oven. Sauté the duck quarters, onion, and garlic until the duck is nicely browned on all sides. Crush some peppercorns, coriander seeds, cumin seeds, and sea salt with a mortar and pestle, or fold them in waxed paper and pound them with a flat mallet. Sprinkle the mixture over the ducks. Add

3 cups of boiling water. Cover tightly and simmer for an hour or so, or until the ducks are tender but not falling off the bone. Remove the duck pieces and set them aside to cool a little. Add the rice to the pan and bring to a new boil. Then reduce the heat, cover tightly, and simmer for 20 minutes. Meanwhile, pull the duck meat from the bones, cut it into bite-size pieces, and add it back to the pot. Simmer uncovered until the liquid has been absorbed by the rice or has evaporated. The dish should be quite moist, but not soupy.

Note: This Peruvian duck recipe came indirectly from a book called *Pre-Hispanic Cooking,* a scholarly work published in Mexico and printed in both English and Spanish. My wife purchased the book for me some time ago at the Smithsonian gift shop in Washington, D.C. Knowing that ducks were domesticated in what is now Latin America long before the Spanish came, I eagerly searched through the pages for an authentic American duck recipe. I'm talking Aztec or Mayan. It was not there. Perhaps, I concluded, the duck was actually domesticated by the Inca down in Peru instead of in Mexico, in which case Pato con Arroz might well be the real stuff, made with quinoa instead of rice.

But my nose for scholarship tells me that I should refrain from drawing too many conclusions from the *Pre-Hispanic Cooking* work. In spite of its scholarly aspect and art cover (a detail from a mural by Diego Rivera showing a topless Indian woman patting out a tortilla), I strongly doubt that the book is accurate on all counts. The recipe for "Ham in Pulque," for example, calls for a Virginia ham, pulque, thyme, oregano, cloves, and even cinnamon. Pulque, an alcoholic brew made from the agave plant, was popular in Mexico both as a beer and as a culinary ingredient long before the Spanish came. Indeed, pulque might well have been used in pre-Hispanic times to cook up javelina, or peccary. But the javelina isn't a real pig or boar. Neither pigs nor the spices listed in the recipe were available in the New World before the Spanish brought them—so where the hell would an Aztec get a Virginia ham?

THREE

Frying Ducks and Geese

Although frying is not the classical way of cooking ducks and geese, don't count it out. Some of the recipes below could fit into the previous chapter on skillet cooking, but remember that frying can also be accomplished in a wok and deep fryer—and sautéing requires only a griddle.

Camp Fried Duck

In my *Complete Fish & Game Cookbook,* I said that the best duck I ever ate was cooked in a skillet on the Pea River back when I was a boy. I hold to the statement here, but I'll have to add that atmosphere and appetite probably had a lot to do with the taste! We had pitched camp on property owned by a large timber-holding corporation, but the local fellow who had put us on a turkey roost seemed to hold some sort of ownership over the woods. In any case, this fellow could cook as well as roost turkey. One night he beat some duck breasts with the mouth of a bottle, salted and peppered them, rolled them in flour, and fried them in peanut oil over a bed of oak coals. At the time I thought they were the best birds I had ever eaten, and since then I have used the same technique on many occasions. The duck breasts can also be pounded with a meat mallet or the edge of a plate. It's best to flour the fillets thinly and fry quickly in hot oil, browning the outside without overcooking the inside. Eat these with your fingers, biting off a mouthful as needed.

Wild Duck with Gravy

Here's a recipe that makes a very good gravy. The measures in the list of ingredients are for a large wild duck, mallard-size. Since the measurements aren't exact, adjustments can easily be made for more ducks or for small ducks. You'll need enough bacon grease for gravy—but not too much.

> wild duck breast fillets
> 2 strips of thick bacon for each large duck
> flour
> salt and pepper
> water

Fillet the duck breasts and tenderize if needed. Fry the bacon in a skillet until crisp. Drain and crumble. Cut the duck breasts into bite-size pieces, then sprinkle them with salt and pepper, shake them in a bag with a little flour, and fry them in hot bacon grease. Drain the duck, leaving some grease in the pan. Add 1 tablespoon of flour to ¼ cup of water, and stir until you have a smooth paste. Add this paste slowly to the grease left in the skillet, stirring as you go with a wooden spoon, until you have gravy of the consistency you like. Add salt and pepper to the gravy to taste, and stir in the crumbled bacon. Serve the gravy over the duck pieces. The gravy also goes nicely over rice, mashed potatoes, or biscuit halves.

Variation: Try some salt pork instead of cured bacon, in which case the salt can be omitted. For serving with baked potatoes, reserve the fried bacon bits or pork cracklings instead of mixing them into the gravy. Spoon some of the gravy over a split and fluffed baked potato, and sprinkle some of the bacon bits or pork cracklings on top.

Stir-Fried Duck

I confess that I really don't have a recipe for stir-fried duck. Although I have cooked variations of the dish many times, the ingredients often depend on what I have on hand. I might use a little hoisin sauce, for example, if I've got some handy, or perhaps Myron's 20-Gauge Wild Game Sauce. Any jackleg stir-fry cook can easily come up with ingredients. Of course, the basic procedure is pretty much the same, provided that the meat is cut thinly or in small chunks. With duck, it's best to use only the breast fillets, which should be sliced thinly across the grain.

1. Heat the oil, then add the oil flavoring, such as ginger root or garlic.

2. Cook the duck (or other meat) and vegetables for a few minutes in hot oil. Drain. Then cook the vegetables.

3. Combine the meat and vegetables. Add the sauce ingredients and, sometimes, a sauce thickener, usually a paste made with cornstarch and a little water. Cover the wok or skillet for 1 or 2 minutes.

Kiwi Duck Breast

As pointed out in chapter 2, the kiwifruit is a powerful natural meat tenderizer, making it a good item to pack for camp cooking, where meats are likely to be on the tough side. It also has a long shelf life, packs compactly, and doesn't break.

duck breast fillets
kiwifruit
butter
flour
red wine
chicken broth or water
salt and pepper

Working one at a time, place the duck fillets on a smooth, flat surface, cover with waxed paper, and pound flat with the smooth side of a meat mallet or some such flat surface. Do this slowly, starting in the middle and working outward, pounding with short strokes. Continue until you have worked the breast down to between ¼ and ⅜ inch. Slice a kiwifruit or two very thinly, using a fillet knife, and shape some slices on a plate roughly the shape of a pounded duck fillet. Place a pounded fillet on the kiwi. Add a layer of kiwifruit slices on top of the fillet, then add a second fillet, and so on, ending with a layer of kiwifruit. Cover and put in a cool place for several hours. When you are ready to cook, melt some butter in a skillet. Sprinkle the fillets with salt and pepper (without rinsing them), then sauté them a few at a time for 1 minute on each side, or until the center of the meat is pinkish. Place the sautéed fillets on a heated serving platter. After all the fillets have been cooked, add some fresh butter to the skillet if needed and stir in a little flour. Cook for several minutes, then stir in some chicken broth or water. Add the wine. Cook over medium heat until you have a nice gravy. Serve with rice and steamed vegetables, along with hot French bread and a salad.

Note: If you have Frenchmen sitting at the table, you might call the gravy sauce and the beaten fillets *paillards.*

Duck Burger

Ground duck meat is very good in spaghetti sauce, chili, casseroles, and burgers. I use a hand-cranked grinder fitted with a ³⁄₁₆-inch wheel. The meat grinds easier if you will chill it and cut it across the grain into small chunks. This recipe, for patties, calls for some ground bacon. Some other uses of ground duck meat, such as spaghetti sauce, will require no fat.

1½ pounds duck meat
½ pound smoked bacon
1 medium onion, finely chopped
salt and pepper
bacon drippings or cooking oil
flour (if needed)
chicken egg (if needed)

Chill or partly freeze the duck meat and bacon, then cut into 1-inch pieces. Mix the pieces together, along with the chopped onion and a little salt and pepper. Grind the mixture in a sausage mill. Shape part of the ground meat into a patty and fry it in some bacon drippings or cooking oil, turning carefully with a spatula. Remove to drain. If the patty has held together, cook the rest of the batch. If not, mix in some flour and a whisked chicken egg. Use the patties to make burgers or, if you prefer, stir up a little gravy with the pan drippings and serve the patties like hamburger steaks.

Golden Fried Duck

This recipe could also go into the chapter on steaming duck and geese. In any case, it is a wonderful dish.

2 mallards
3 tablespoons soy sauce
1 tablespoon sake, sherry, or dry vermouth
4 green onions with tops, chopped
4 slices ginger root, chopped
4 whole star anise
1 teaspoon Szechuan peppercorns, crushed
peanut oil for deep frying
water
salt and freshly ground black pepper

Pluck, draw, and rinse the ducks. Place them in a nonmetallic bowl or a large zip bag. Mix the wine, star anise, green onions, ginger, and Szechuan peppercorns. Pour the mixture over the duck, turning to coat all sides. Marinate for 1 or 2 hours. Rig for steaming. Place the birds over boiling water for 45 minutes. While waiting, rig for deep frying at 375 degrees. After steaming the ducks, brush them heavily with soy sauce. Drain for 15 minutes. Carefully place the ducks into the hot oil for a few minutes, until they are golden brown. Drain on brown bags or other absorbent paper. Cut the birds into pieces. Serve hot, along with salt and freshly ground black pepper.

Golden Fried Goose

Follow the recipe above, increasing the steaming time to 1½ hours for a 5- to 6-pound goose (dressed weight). An old goose should be steamed longer, until tender. Increase the frying time a little, until the bird is golden brown and the skin crispy.

Fried Snow Goose

Here's a recipe for frying a snow goose, young or old. Skin the bird, draw it, and cut it into serving pieces similar to chicken. The thighs are especially good when cooked by this recipe. Fry the giblets also.

> 1 snow goose
> finely chopped onion
> peanut oil
> flour
> salt and pepper
> water

Salt and pepper the goose pieces, then shake them in a bag with a little flour. Heat ¾ inch of oil in a large skillet. Brown the goose pieces, turning once, and drain. Sauté the chopped onion. Pour off most of the oil. Put the goose pieces back into the skillet with the onion. Add about 1 cup of water. Bring to a boil, reduce the heat to very low, cover, and barely simmer for 1 hour, or until the goose is very tender. Add a little more water from time to time, and turn the pieces to prevent burning on the bottom. Serve the gravy over rice, mashed potatoes, or biscuit halves. Feeds 2 to 4.

Fred's Fried Sea Duck

Sea ducks aren't normally fried—but here's a recipe from *The Maine Way,* attributed to Fred Kircheis of Carmel.

"For each person, use the breast meat from 1 scoter, 1 eider, or 2 old squaws. It is important to remove all traces of fat, skin, and bloodshot meat. Slice into ½ inch thick steaks (each duck = 4 slices). Soak in salted water overnight. Drain and pat dry with paper towel. Shake pieces in mixture of flour, salt, and pepper. Fry in butter as you prefer steak (rare, medium, etc.). This recipe makes fine eating out of a fine game bird."

FOUR

Ducks and Geese in the Big Pot

Pot cooking comes to perfection with long, slow simmering instead of boiling. A cast-iron Dutch oven, designed for stove-top cooking, is my personal choice. I also insist on a tight-fitting cast-iron lid, dome-shaped with little tits arranged geometrically on the inside. Why? Even when cooking at a simmer, water vapor rises from the contents of the pot, condenses on the lid, collects on the tits, and drips down all over the breast of the duck or venison roast. This is called self-basting.

Of course, other kinds of pots can be used. Remember, however, that a thick pot that distributes heat evenly isn't as likely to burn the bottom of the food as a thin-skinned pot.

This chapter also includes a few recipes for a Crock-Pot, which is ideal for cooking meats and vegetables for long periods of time—8 or 9 hours. By Crock-Pot I mean those ceramic utensils with an electrical heating element wound around the sides instead of being in the bottom. The side-heated pots are less likely to burn the food and are, in general, almost foolproof. If I had to choose a single cooking device for all sorts of wild game and fowl, a Crock-Pot would be my choice, although I would miss my skillet a lot. And my stove-top Dutch oven.

Another kind of pot used in this chapter is the pressure cooker. These do a good job of tenderizing meat in a short period of time. Although I prefer long, slow simmering to pressure cooking, I should point out that the pressure cooker is by far the best choice at high altitudes, where the moisture cooks out of meat at temperatures of less than 212 degrees. In other words, the pressure cooker helps get the food done without drying it out. Most of these units come with an instruction booklet, which should be followed closely.

Brazilian Duck

The duck was one of the three animals that were domesticated for food in the Americas, the others being the wild turkey and the guinea pig. Of course, the Indians of both North and South America also had plenty of wild ducks to hunt. In any case, this recipe works with two mallard-size birds.

> 2 large wild ducks
> 2 slices cured bacon or salt pork
> 2 tablespoons butter
> 1 medium onion, diced
> 1 cup small Portuguese green olives
> 1 tablespoon chopped fresh celery leaves
> 1 tablespoon chopped fresh parsley
> 4 to 8 whole green chili peppers
> 1 bay leaf
> salt to taste
> 2 cups boiling water
> flour paste

Pluck the birds and disjoint them, cutting the breast in half and separating the leg and thigh. (Use the back, neck, and wings for soup or stock.) Fry the bacon in a stove-top Dutch oven until done. Remove the bacon and add the butter to the grease. Brown the duck pieces. Add the onion and cook for 5 minutes. Then add the boiling water, whole chili peppers, bay leaf, parsley, celery tops, and salt. Cover tightly and simmer until the duck is very tender, turning from time to time and adding more water if needed.

While the duck simmers, cut each olive in an unbroken spiral and have these ready. When the duck is done, remove the pieces to a serving platter. Also remove the peppers intact and discard them, or save them for any of your guests who like hot stuff. Thicken the gravy with the flour paste, made by stirring a little flour into 2 tablespoons of cold water; add the paste slowly, stirring as you go, until the gravy is thickened. Scald the olives in boiling water for 2 minutes. Serve the gravy over the duck pieces, topping with the blanched olive spirals.

This duck goes nicely with rice and steamed vegetables, perhaps topped with crumbled bacon. Try chayote (*xu-xu* in Brazil). For a real treat, serve the dish with Brazilian hearts of palm, available in the can; in rural Florida, this delicacy is called swamp cabbage. Also, remember that fiddleheads (unopened fern fronds) are popular in Brazil, and these can sometimes be purchased in specialized markets or picked from the wild in the spring.

Be warned that the hot peppers listed in the recipe above should not be cut up. If you do cut into them, be sure to remove the seeds and inner pith. Otherwise, the dish may be too hot to suit your guests.

Turkish Two-Pot Duck

This is an old Turkish recipe for duck, adapted here from Claudia Roden's *A Book of Middle Eastern Food.* You'll need two Dutch ovens or other suitable pots for cooking this recipe.

> 2 or 3 mallards or ducks of similar size
> duck giblets
> 2½ cups long-grain rice
> ½ cup plain yogurt
> ½ cup raisins
> ⅓ cup pine nuts
> 2 medium onions, chopped
> oil or butter
> salt and pepper

Dress the birds, saving the giblets, and cut into serving pieces. Add a little salt to the yogurt. Toss the duck pieces with the yogurt to coat all sides, then refrigerate for several hours. Drain.

In a Dutch oven or other suitable pot, sauté the onions in a little oil or butter until golden. Add more oil if needed and brown the duck pieces. Cover with water, add the duck gizzards and hearts along with a little salt and pepper, and bring to a boil. Then reduce the heat and simmer for 1 hour, or until tender. Remove the duck pieces to drain and reserve 5 cups of stock. If you don't have 5 cups, make up the difference with water.

Chop the cooked gizzards and hearts, as well as the uncooked liver. Sauté these in a little butter in another Dutch oven or suitable pot. Add the pine nuts, raisins, salt, pepper, and reserved duck stock. Bring to a boil, add the rice, reduce the heat, cover, and cook without peeking for 20 minutes. Serve on a heated platter, alternating layers of rice and duck. Feeds 6.

Justin Wilson's Duck and Turnips

Sometimes a topic is so germane to the larger subject that it is overlooked by people who prepare the indexes to books. While thumbing through Justin Wilson's *Gourmet and Gourmand*, for example, I stopped at a recipe called "Duck and Turnips." The rich, dark meat of duck goes nicely with turnip roots, and I was therefore compelled to test the recipe. The directions said, "Make a roux with the flour and oil (see my recipe)." Naturally, I looked in the index for Wilson's recipe for roux, and found no entry by that name. I flipped back and forth in the book, and finally went to the table of contents for a clue. "How to Make a Roux" was the name of the first chapter! In any case, I have worked the roux ritual into the directions below, and I have otherwise finagled with the recipe to suit my own style. In short, Wilson may not "garontee" the results.

To cook the dish, I use a stove-top Dutch oven and a large cast-iron skillet.

3 or 4 ducks, mallard-size
8 cups coarsely chopped turnip roots
3 cups chopped onions
1 cup chopped red bell pepper
1 cup chopped green onions with part of tops
1 cup chopped celery with part of tops
1 cup chopped fresh parsley
3 cloves minced garlic
1 lemon, seeded and minced
1 cup plain flour
½ cup cooking oil or bacon drippings
4 to 6 cups water
3 cups dry white wine
1 tablespoon Worcestershire sauce
1 tablespoon Louisiana hot sauce (or Tabasco)
1 tablespoon soy sauce
1 teaspoon dried mint, crushed
½ teaspoon Peychaud's bitters
salt

Heat the oil or bacon drippings in the skillet. Add the flour, reduce to very low heat, and stir lovingly for an hour with a wooden spoon, making a dark brown roux. If you are in a hurry, ask your wife to stir the roux while you get on with the rest of the cooking. Skin, draw, and bone the ducks, then cut the meat into 2-inch cubes. (Save the bony parts for stock or soup.) Brown the ducks in a little oil in a Dutch oven. Into the roux, stir the chopped onions, green onions, parsley, garlic, celery, and red bell pepper, simmering for about 5 minutes. Stir in 4 cups of water, wine, Worcestershire sauce, soy sauce, bitters, dried mint, Louisiana hot sauce, chopped lemon, and salt. Mix the chopped turnips into the duck in the Dutch oven. Then pour the contents of the skillet into the duck and turnips. Cover tightly and simmer on low for 4 or 5 hours, adding a little more water if needed.

Note: Don't let the long list of ingredients put you off. Any Cajun recipe with less than twenty ingredients and no cross references is worth a shot, so be sure to try this one. I might add that many other recipes, going back to the ancient Romans, call for stewing duck with turnip roots. Many European recipes still can be made with this combination.

Cacciatore Garigliana

This recipe has been adapted from *Game and Fish Cookbook,* by Harriet and James Barnett. The authors say they got it from a fellow by the name of Ray Camp, who at one time wrote an outdoors column for the *New York Times.* Camp, in turn, got the recipe while in Italy during World War II. The Barnetts say it is particularly delicious, and I agree. The original called for cooking the dish in a large glazed earthenware pot. I don't have such a pot, and if I did have one I would hesitate to put it atop direct heat from the stove. Instead, I use my cast-iron stove-top Dutch oven. The recipe called for 2 cups of red wine and 1 cup of white wine. Because I usually have to buy the wine especially for the recipe, I use 3 cups of red wine or rosé. Rich people and Italians might want to use both red and white *vino.* The recipe also calls for a small pinch of saffron. I don't usually list ingredients in dashes or pinches, but anyone who prices this stuff won't have a problem with the measure. If you don't have a small pinch of saffron, try a large pinch of powdered turmeric.

3 wild ducks, mallard-size
¾ cup olive oil
3 ripe tomatoes, diced
3 large onions, diced
1 carrot, scraped and diced
2 small tart apples, peeled, cored, and diced
4 cloves garlic, minced
3 cups dry red wine
½ teaspoon oregano
small pinch of saffron
salt and freshly ground black pepper

Pluck the ducks and quarter them, then sprinkle them with salt and pepper. Heat the olive oil in the Dutch oven. A few pieces at a time, sauté the duck quarters until lightly browned. Drain the duck and set aside. Sauté the onions until lightly browned, then add the carrot, tomatoes, apples, garlic, oregano, saffron, wine, salt, and pepper. Bring to a simmer, then add the pieces of duck. Cover tightly and simmer for 2 or 3 hours. I serve this dish with regular white rice or wild rice, but the Barnetts call for saffron rice cooked as directed in chapter 11 (see Saffron Pilau).

Gulf City Duck

Here's a historical recipe from *Gulf City Cook Book,* published in Mobile, Alabama, in 1878. It might be the first of thousands of committee-written books published for charity, having been compiled by "The Ladies of the St. Francis Street Methodist Episcopal Church." Back then, recipe writers were a little short on details, and I assume that the "dressing" used in the recipe is indeed dressing instead of stuffing. Although most of the ladies probably didn't hunt, wild ducks from Mobile Bay and elsewhere were available at market. Canvasbacks were plentiful, the hunting good. The food, too. Anyhow, here's the recipe:

"Prepare your dressing as you would for any other fowl, with the addition of more onion. Dry the ducks, sprinkle with salt and pepper, and roll in flour. Take three or four whole onions, put all in a pan with hot lard; turn frequently, until brown; add water enough to cover the fowls. Cook until there is just enough liquor left for the gravy."

Note: I might add that this is an easy dish to prepare in camp, using a Dutch oven loaded with 2 mallard-size birds.

Duck and Daylilies

Daylilies, both the buds and flowers, are used in Chinese cookery and should be used more often in America. The young buds are very good in stir-fry dishes, and should be tried in the Stir-Fried Duck recipe (chapter 3). The blossoms are also good and are sold dried in some Chinese markets. If you have a bed of daylilies, or have a friend who does, then pick your own. I always pick them just before sundown of the first day of bloom, when they start to wilt. Thus, picking them won't detract from the beauty of the plant, as the spent blooms quickly fall to the ground.

I have adapted this recipe from Leona Woodring Smith's *The Forgotten Art of Flower Cookery*, which says, "The Chinese enjoyed the day lily long before the written word, and earliest records tell of the plant's use as food. An herbal from the T'ang Dynasty, about A.D. 650, informs us that 'it quiets the five viscera [lungs, kidneys, stomach, intestines, and liver], reduces worry, and benefits the mind.'"

>1 large wild duck, cut into pieces
>2 cups daylily blossoms, chopped
>1 cup sliced mushrooms
>1 medium onion
>4 tablespoons butter
>3 tablespoons peanut butter
>2 tablespoons cornstarch
>2 tablespoons soy sauce
>1 tablespoon grated orange rind
>1 tablespoon grated fresh ginger
>½ teaspoon nutmeg
>1 bay leaf
>salt and pepper
>cloves

Put the duck into a Dutch oven (or suitable pot), and cover it with water. Stud the onion with cloves, then put it into the pot, along with a bay leaf and a little salt. Simmer for 45 minutes. Drain the duck, patting it dry with paper towels. Strain and reserve 2½ cups of the stock, discarding the onion, cloves, and bay leaf. Sauté the duck in butter until it is golden brown. Remove the duck to a heated serving platter. Mix the cornstarch and soy sauce, adding it to the Dutch oven; simmer and stir with a wooden spoon until the sauce thickens. Add the peanut butter, nutmeg, ginger, orange rind, salt, and pepper. Bring to a simmer, add the mushrooms and daylilies, and cook for 4 minutes. Pour the sauce over the duck. Serve hot with rice and steamed Chinese vegetables, or perhaps with stir-fried vegetables, including a few daylily buds.

New England Braised Wild Duck

Here's an old New England recipe, best cooked in a stove-top Dutch oven or similar pot.

> 1 large wild duck or 2 small ones
> 4 slices bacon
> 1 large onion, sliced
> 1 carrot, sliced
> 4 tablespoons brown sugar
> 2 tablespoons orange juice
> juice of 1 lemon
> zest of 1 lemon
> 1 tablespoon fresh parsley
> 1 teaspoon fresh thyme
> salt and pepper

Clean and disjoint the duck, rub the pieces with the lemon juice, and sprinkle with salt and pepper. Fry the bacon in the Dutch oven. Remove and crumble the bacon. Sear the duck pieces in the hot bacon drippings, then sauté the onion and carrot. Drain off the fat. Add the parsley and thyme to the pot, then sprinkle everything with the brown sugar, crumbled bacon, lemon zest, and orange juice, along with any remaining lemon juice. Cover tightly and simmer for 30 minutes. Serve hot.

Easy Goose & Cabbage

The people of Europe are fond of eating duck and geese with cabbage or sauerkraut. Here's an easy recipe from Yugoslavia, where it is cooked with domestic geese. It works just as well with large Canadas. It's an easy dish, but it is best cooked first in a roasting pan in the oven and then on top of the stove in a large pot. Most stove-top Dutch ovens are ideal.

> 1 wild goose
> 3 heads cabbage, finely chopped
> 3 large onions, sliced
> salt and pepper
> olive oil or goose grease

Preheat the oven to 450 degrees. Cut the goose into serving pieces. Roast in a suitable pan for about 20 minutes, then reduce the heat to 350 degrees and cook until tender, about 1 hour. In a stove-top Dutch oven, heat 3 tablespoons of olive oil or goose grease. Sauté the onion slices until they are golden, then add the chopped cabbage. Top the cabbage with the goose pieces, salt, and pepper. Cover tightly and simmer on very low heat for 1 hour.

Chinese-Style Canada Goose

This old Chinese recipe for large Peking duck is one of my favorite ways to cook a wild goose.

> 1 Canada goose
> 2 cups water
> 1 cup soy sauce
> ½ cup sake, vermouth, or sherry
> 6 green onions with tops, chopped
> 4 slices fresh ginger root
> 4 whole star anise
> 4 cloves
> 1 stick cinnamon
> 2 tablespoons sugar
> ½ teaspoon black pepper

Mix all the ingredients except the goose in a large pot. Add the goose, breast down. Bring to a boil, then lower the heat, cover tightly, and simmer for 45 minutes. Turn the goose, cover tightly, and simmer for another 45 minutes. Remove and drain the goose. Strain the pot liquid, discarding all the solids. Bring the liquid to a boil in a saucepan and reduce by half, making a thin sauce. When the goose has cooled down, cut it into bite-size pieces and serve it with a little of the sauce. Serve with lots of rice and steamed vegetables.

Crock-Pot Ducks

The Crock-Pot is one of my favorite ways of cooking game, and it works nicely with ducks, young or old. The measures for this recipe aren't exact, and a good deal depends on the size of your Crock-Pot. For a medium-size Crock-Pot (by far the most common), you'll need at least 2 mallards or the equivalent. It is important that the pot be filled to the top, or almost to the top, with something good and compatible with the dish. I usually cap the pot off with mushrooms.

> 2 mallards or several smaller ducks
> 8 or 10 new potatoes, golf-ball size
> 2 cups chopped carrots
> 2 cups diced onion
> mushrooms as needed
> ½ cup red wine
> 3 bay leaves
> salt and pepper

Fillet the duck breasts and cut out the leg and thigh, saving the rest of the bird for soup. Place the carrots, duck pieces, bay leaves, potatoes, onion, mushrooms, salt, pepper, and wine into the Crock-Pot, in that order. Cover, turn the heat to low, and cook for 8 or 9 hours. Serve hot, spooning the gravy over rice or noodles. Feeds 4 to 6.

Crock-Pot Goose Thighs

The Crock-Pot is a good way to cook goose thighs and legs, saving the breast and bony parts for other recipes. You can also mix in duck legs and thighs.

> legs and thighs from several geese and ducks
> chopped onions
> chopped green onion tops or chives
> mushrooms
> ½ cup red wine
> ½ cup orange marmalade
> 3 bay leaves
> salt and pepper

Skin the goose quarters, separate them into legs and thighs, and layer them in the Crock-Pot. Add the onions, green onion tops, and bay leaves. Top off with mushrooms, filling the pot, or almost so. Sprinkle with salt and pepper. Spread the orange marmalade on top, then pour in the wine. Cook on low heat for 8 or 9 hours. Serve the meat and gravy with rice and vegetables, along with the rest of the red wine and some hot sourdough biscuits or French bread.

Pressure-Cooked Duck

If properly used, the pressure cooker can save lots of time and still produce succulent meat. Here's a basic recipe that I hope will come in handy from time to time.

> 2 mallard-size ducks
> ½ cup olive oil
> 1 cup red wine
> lemon-pepper seasoning salt

Pluck, draw, and disjoint the duck, cutting it into serving-size pieces. Dry the pieces and sprinkle them on both sides with lemon-pepper seasoning salt. Heat the olive oil in the pressure cooker on high heat, then brown the duck pieces on both sides, cooking several batches. Drain the duck pieces and pour the oil out of the cooker. Put the browned duck pieces back into the cooker. Add the wine and cover, locking the lid. Attach the 15-pound regulator. Put the pot on high heat. As soon as the regulator starts steaming, reduce the heat and cook for 15 minutes. Remove the cooker from the heat and let cool naturally. Remove the duck pieces to a serving platter and pour the pan juices over them.

Variations: Use water instead of wine. After the ducks are done, remove them to a serving platter. Stir a little flour into the pan drippings to make a paste. Stir in ½ cup of Grand Marnier and ½ cup of orange meats, obtained by peeling an orange, breaking it into sections, peeling the sections, and discarding the seeds. Heat for a few minutes. Serve the gravy with the duck pieces. It's easy to come up with other variations for the gravy.

Wild Goose with Chestnuts

Here's a recipe that works when you've got a mixed bag of large and small geese, young and old. It's best to use thighs or perhaps a combination of thighs and breast fillets, saving the other pieces for soup. I cook the dish in a large stove-top Dutch oven.

> 8 pounds goose thighs and breast fillets
> 2 pounds chestnuts
> 1 cup beef stock
> 1 cup dry wine, red or white
> ¼ cup butter
> ¼ cup olive oil
> 4 carrots, minced
> 1 rib celery with tops, minced
> 2 medium onions, minced
> 2 cloves garlic, minced
> 2 tablespoons tomato paste
> 2 tablespoons fresh chopped parsley
> 2 bay leaves
> 1 tablespoon fresh thyme
> salt and pepper
> boiling water

In a large stove-top Dutch oven, heat the oil and butter. Cook the goose pieces, a few at a time, until golden. Remove the pieces to drain. Sauté the onion, garlic, carrots, and celery. Add the goose pieces back to the pot, along with the beef broth, wine, tomato paste, salt, pepper, parsley, bay leaves, and thyme. Add just enough boiling water to cover the goose pieces. Bring to a boil, then reduce the heat, cover, and simmer for 2 hours, stirring a time or two so that the bottom won't burn. While waiting, shuck the chestnuts. After 2 hours, add the chestnuts to the pot, cover, and simmer for 30 to 40 minutes. Arrange the goose pieces on a heated serving platter, with the chestnuts at either end or in a separate container. Spoon the gravy from the pot over the goose pieces and chestnuts. Feeds 8 to 16.

FIVE

Steamed and Simmered Ducks and Geese

Steamed duck, as such, is not the American way. It's Chinese. Nor is stewed duck very popular in America these days, although it was frequently used in times past, based partly on French and European dishes. I highly recommend both methods, and offer the recipes below. Also, remember that ducks that are baked or roasted in a bag or wrapped in aluminum foil are essentially steamed, and that some of the big pot dishes in chapter 4 as well as some of the skillet dishes in chapter 2 could easily fit into this chapter under the simmered category.

Steamed Duck, Chinese-Style

Fortunately, here is a very good recipe from Nanking, adapted from Maggie Gin's *Regional Cooking of China,* that doesn't call for lots of esoteric ingredients. The hardest part about this recipe is in getting rigged up for steaming. If you've got a bamboo steamer, you're in business. If not, you'll need a pot with a rack inside and a tight lid.

>   4 pounds dressed duck
>   5 tablespoons sea salt, crushed
>   1 tablespoon Szechuan peppercorns, crushed
>   2 green onions with tops
>   2 tablespoons sake

Place the crushed peppercorns and salt in a small cast-iron skillet. Heat and stir until the salt turns golden. Dry the duck with paper towels and rub it inside and out with the salt mixture. Refrigerate the duck overnight.

When you are ready to cook, rinse the duck quickly. Pat it dry with paper towels and place it on a heatproof dish. Rig for steaming and turn on the heat. Chop the green onions and place them inside the duck. Rub the outside with sake. Place the duck (on the dish) into the steamer and close the lid tightly. Steam wild ducks for 30 to 45 minutes, depending on the size. Take the steamer off the heat and let it stand for 30 minutes, covered. Remove the duck. Bone the duck and cut it into bite-size pieces. Discard the onions from the duck cavity. Pour the juices from the steaming dish over the duck pieces and serve with rice and steamed or stir-fried vegetables.

A Double-Barreled Duck Recipe

Myron Becker, the originator of Myron's 20 Gauge Wild Game Sauce, sent me this recipe, explaining, "It came about by accident. At one of our game feasts 5 or 6 years ago, we were going to make smoked duck (a mixture of mallards, blacks, and a few eider), but we ended up with something different and in my opinion spectacular. . . . OK. First, here's my recipe for smoked ducks." Then Myron set forth the ingredients and details pretty much as follows. He didn't specify the number of ducks, but, by my reckoning, the curing ingredients will treat at least 3 or 4 birds. Mix a larger batch if needed.

3 or 4 ducks
1 cup brown sugar
1 cup kosher salt
2 tablespoons minced fresh ginger root
2 tablespoons minced or pressed garlic
1 tablespoon Szechuan peppercorns
1 tablespoon ground star anise
apple wood
grapevine

In a dry skillet, heat the peppercorns and star anise until fragrant. Mix the peppercorns, anise, brown sugar, salt, ginger, and garlic. Pluck, draw, and wash the ducks, then pat them dry. Rub them inside and out with the curing mix, then pack them in the curing mix in a nonmetallic container. Let sit overnight. Wash the birds and hang them in a cool, airy place until a pellicle forms (that is, until the skin is dry and takes on a shellacked look). Smoke for 4 to 6 hours at a temperature not to exceed 160 degrees, using a mixture of water-soaked grapevine and apple wood.

"However," Myron went on, "by the time the ducks had been cured and dried, we had had a bit too much to drink to get it together with the smoker. So instead, we slow steamed them in a large covered wok using a small puddle of sake with garlic, ginger, Szechuan peppercorns, and star anise as the liquid. After steaming the ducks for 2 or 3 hours, we removed them and sliced the meat thinly. Then we skimmed the liquor left in the wok, reduced it to sauce consistency, added some chopped cilantro, and drizzled it over the sliced duck. The effect was almost like a fine prosciutto with a Southeast Asian influence."

A. D.'s Kumquat Duck with Leftovers

Although the kumquat resembles a small orange or satsuma, it is really not a member of the citrus family. The peel is really the best part, at least to me, and is sweeter than the insides. In any case, this fruit of the Orient goes nicely with duck and geese, and I like to use some along with a little soy sauce. My recipe is designed to feed 4 people for 2 meals. It's best to fill the Crock-Pot to the top, and the number of ducks required depends on their size. Of course, it also depends on the size of the Crock-Pot. I almost always use one with a 3½-quart capacity. Use the breasts, drumsticks, and thighs for this recipe, saving the rest for soup or stock cooked separately.

duck breasts, legs, and thighs
20 to 30 kumquats
3 tablespoons soy sauce
1 tablespoon Grand Marnier
freshly ground black pepper
plum or duck sauce (for day 1)
water or chicken stock (if needed for day 2)
rice (cooked separately)

Fill the Crock-Pot about one-third full with duck pieces, then add about a third of the kumquats (whole). Add another layer of ducks and kumquats; repeat, ending with kumquats. Sprinkle with pepper, then pour in the soy sauce and Grand Marnier. Cook on low heat for 9 hours.

For the first meal, remove and bone the duck breasts. Slice the meat crosswise, then serve hot along with Chinese plum sauce (sometimes called duck sauce), rice, steamed vegetables, and a few of the kumquats.

For the second day, remove and bone the duck pieces. Chop the meat, then put it and the remaining kumquats into the refrigerator in a suitable covered container. Pour the Crock-Pot liquid into a widemouthed jar and refrigerate. When you are ready to cook, remove all fat from the top of the stock (it will have formed a solid white layer). Melt the stock in a skillet. Remove the seeds from the kumquats, then slice the skin and pulp. Stir the kumquats and duck meat into the stock. The mix should be on the verge of soupiness, so add a little water or chicken stock if needed. Heat through and serve hot over rice. Note that the makings for the second meal can be kept for a few days in the refrigerator, or frozen for later use.

Creole Stewed Duck

Here's an old New Orleans recipe for stewing duck, which was a popular method among turn-of-the-century Creole cooks. It's just as good today. This recipe and the next one were adapted from *The Picayune Creole Cook Book,* second edition, first published in 1901.

2 large wild ducks
½ cup finely diced ham
2 medium onions, chopped
2 cloves garlic, minced
1 cup chopped fresh mushrooms
1 cup water
1 cup claret
1 tablespoon butter
1 tablespoon chopped fresh thyme
1 tablespoon chopped fresh parsley
2 bay leaves
salt and freshly ground pepper

Pluck, singe, draw, and disjoint the birds, saving the bony pieces for soup or stock. Rub the pieces with salt and pepper. Heat the butter in a deep pot or Dutch oven, then sauté the onions and mushrooms until they brown a little. Add the ducks, turning to sear all sides. Add the chopped ham, claret, garlic, thyme, parsley, and bay leaves. Simmer for 10 minutes, stirring often. Add the water, cover, and simmer for 1 hour, stirring from time to time and adding more water if needed. Serve hot, spooning the gravy over rice, along with some New Orleans or French bread and vegetables.

Also see the next recipe.

Stewed Duck with Turnips

Turnips go nicely with duck, and the combination has been served since the time of Apicus, the Roman culinary sport. Follow the recipe above, but omit the mushrooms and claret. After adding the diced ham, peel and quarter 6 turnips and add to the pot. Also add 1 tablespoon flour, stirring well. Then add the thyme, parsley, bay leaves, and minced garlic. Cook for about 15 minutes, stirring constantly. Then add enough water to almost cover the duck parts. Bring to a boil, reduce the heat, and simmer for ½ hour. Serve hot.

Duck Salad

This recipe can be used with leftover duck, but it's really better to simmer a whole bird for it. Also try making it with a pair of goose leg quarters.

> 1 large wild duck
> 1 large onion, chopped
> 2 ribs celery with tops, chopped
> 2 hard-boiled chicken eggs
> ¼ cup chopped pecans
> mayonnaise
> bay leaf
> salt and pepper

Skin and draw the duck. Put it into a pot, along with the giblets, cover with water, add a bay leaf, and simmer for 1½ hours, or until the meat is very tender. Bone and chop the meat and giblets, and mix with the onion, celery, chopped eggs, pecans, mayonnaise, salt, and pepper. As a salad, serve on lettuce leaves. Also use the mixture as a sandwich spread, or serve with crackers as a snack.

SIX

Grilling and Smoking Ducks and Geese

For true grilling, meat is cooked directly over the heat, be it from charcoal, wood coals, gas, or electric elements. The intensity of the heat, the thickness of the meat, the distance from the heat to the surface of the meat, and the cooking time are all very important. The ideal is to cook the surface of the meat to a nice color while leaving the inside quite moist and succulent. To this end, thin pieces of meat should be cooked quite close to high heat for a short period of time. Large chunks of meat should be cooked some distance from the heat for a longer period of time. Thus, grilling is not an exact science. I wouldn't call it an art, but I will say that experience is the best guide.

Smoking is often accomplished along with the grilling. If the meat is cooked directly over the heat, the drippings from the meat or the basting sauce will provide some smoke. Wood chips are also used to make smoke for flavor. The best smoke, in my opinion, comes from freshly cut hardwood, but there are other opinions on this matter. For convenience, most people buy wood in bags and soak it in water before using it.

Meat that is cooked with the indirect method under a closed hood isn't truly grilled, being cooked partly by baking. It can be very, very good, especially when cooked in connection with wood smoke. The type of grill is important, and each size and shape of grill is different. The ultimate in this category, as I see it, is the two-barrel rig, with a meat rack fitted in the large barrel and a heat source used in the small barrel. Usually, the small barrel is lower than the large one so that the smoke will draw nicely. In any case, the accomplished backyard chef can make good use of wild ducks and geese for both grilling and smoking. Just remember that the meat should not be dried out during the cooking process.

Easy Grilled Duck

As a rule, small ducks are easier than larger ones to grill satisfactorily. In either case, it's best to split the ducks in half. Small ducks can be grilled close to a hot fire, but larger ones have to be cooked more slowly so that the inside will get done before the outside burns. I like ducks cooked over wood coals, but charcoal, gas, or electric heat also works fine.

> mallards or smaller ducks
> olive oil
> minced garlic
> oregano
> salt and pepper
> fresh lemon juice

Build the fire. While waiting for hot coals, rub the duck halves with olive oil and minced garlic. Sprinkle with oregano, salt, and pepper. Grill over a hot fire until done to your liking. Shortly before serving, sprinkle the duck halves lightly with lemon juice.

Good Ol' Boy Ducks

Here's a recipe that works for ducks, dove, and other rich, dark meat cooked on the grill. It's well-nigh foolproof!

     duck breasts
     Italian salad dressing
     red wine
     bacon
     lemon-pepper seasoning salt
     salted water

Skin the duck breasts and soak them overnight in lightly salted water. Rinse and cut the breasts into kabob-size chunks, put them into a nonmetallic container, pour in a little red wine and well-mixed Italian salad dressing, and marinate for 2 hours. Rig for grilling over charcoal or on a gas or electric unit. Wrap each duck piece in half a strip of bacon, secured with a round toothpick, and sprinkle with lemon-pepper. Cook close to the coals for 4 or 5 minutes or so on each side, turning and moving about from time to time with tongs. Cook until the bacon is browned and ready to eat.

Note: Be warned that cooking this recipe is a full-time job, as the dripping bacon grease causes flare-ups that can burn the meat.

Duck Breasts Teriyaki

I use duck fillets, skin on, for this recipe. Save the rest for other recipes, soup, or stock.

     8 breast fillets from large wild duck
     1 cup soy sauce
     3 slices fresh ginger root
     3 cloves garlic, minced
     2 tablespoons Chinese sesame oil
     2 tablespoons sake, dry sherry, or dry vermouth
     1 tablespoon brown sugar

Mix all the ingredients except the duck pieces to make a marinade. Put the duck pieces into a nonmetallic container, add the marinade, and place in the refrigerator for at least 4 hours or overnight. Build a hot charcoal fire in the grill, adjusting the rack to about 4 inches above the coals. While waiting for the grill to heat, drain the duck pieces and pour the leftover marinade into a saucepan. Heat and simmer until the volume is reduced by one-third. Discard the ginger slices. Grill the duck fillets over hot coals for 2 or 3 minutes on each side. Slice the duck breasts. Pour some of the sauce over the sliced meat and serve the rest in a bowl. Serve with rice, fruit, vegetables, and hot bread. Feeds 2 to 4.

Caspian Sea Duck Kabobs

The people in Azerbaijan and other lands in the Caucasus and Caspian area are fond of a tart syrup made with pomegranate juice. The last batch that I bought, imported from Lebanon, was called pomegranate molasses.

> 2 pounds duck breasts
> 2 medium onions, grated
> 2 medium onions, quartered
> 1 lemon, quartered
> 2 or 3 green onions with tops
> ½ cup fresh parsley, chopped
> ¼ cup melted butter
> ¼ cup red wine vinegar
> pomegranate syrup
> rice (cooked separately)
> salt and pepper

Mix the grated onions, salt, pepper, chopped parsley, green onions, lemon quarters, and wine vinegar in a nonmetallic container. Cut the duck breasts into kabob-size pieces, put them in the container, and stir them about to coat all sides. Refrigerate for several hours, stirring from time to time with a wooden spoon.

Rig for grilling over a hot charcoal fire or wood coals. Thread the duck pieces onto skewers, alternating each piece with a segment of the onion quarters. Grill about 4 inches from hot coals on an uncovered grid for 4 or 5 minutes on each side. During the last minute, baste lightly all around with pomegranate syrup and melted butter. Serve over rice, along with grilled eggplant or other grilled vegetables and fruits.

Grill-Ahead Duck

Here's a good recipe to use whenever you are having a guest or two for dinner and don't know the exact time of arrival. Or at any other time, for that matter.

> 2 wild ducks
> 1 can cream of celery soup (10¾-ounce size)
> 2 tablespoons soy sauce
> lemon-pepper seasoning salt
> bacon drippings

Heat up the grill and rig for smoking with wood chips. Rub the duck inside and out with bacon drippings, then sprinkle with lemon-pepper seasoning salt. Grill the ducks under closed hood for about 1 hour, or until the ducks are medium rare. Place the birds in a plastic roasting bag, add the soup and soy sauce, and put into a 400-degree oven for 10 minutes, then reduce the heat to 200 degrees. Leave in the oven for 1 hour—or until serving time. Be sure to save the gravy for the rice.

Campfire Duck

All you need to cook this duck is some heavy-duty aluminum foil and some hot coals. It can be cooked on the patio grill, in the home fireplace, or on a campfire. It's best to rake the coals away from the fire. The fact that this kind of cooking is closer to steaming than to grilling doesn't make it less tasty.

4 to 6 duck breast fillets (from 2 or 3 ducks)
¼ cup butter or bacon drippings
2 medium onions, sliced
salt and pepper

Build a large fire to make lots of coals. Lay a sheet of heavy-duty aluminum foil on a flat surface. Place a layer of onion slices on the foil, then place the duck breast fillets over the onion. Cup the edges of the foil inward. Sprinkle the duck with salt and pepper, and pour on the butter or bacon drippings. Top with another sheet of aluminum foil, fold in 1 inch all around, then make a fold in the first fold, sealing the package. Punch a few small holes in the top. Rake out a bed of hot coals and carefully place the foil packet on them, with the onions on the bottom. Cook for 30 minutes. Open the foil packet, remove the duck, and place the pieces on a platter or plate, top with the onions, and spoon on some of the juices from the foil. The onions can be burned a little on the bottom. Serve with rice and available vegetables. Feeds 2 to 4, depending on how much rice you've cooked.

Variation: If you've got some wild edible mushrooms on hand, slice some and place them on top of the duck pieces.

Angolan Duck with Grilled Papaya

The Portuguese colonized both Angola and Brazil, and the influence of West Africa has helped shape the cuisine of Brazil. But it works the other way, too, and tropical American peppers, fruits, and vegetables became very important in Angola and all of West Central Africa. This recipe reflects that influence.

The Birds
2 mallards, plucked and quartered
½ cup fresh orange juice
½ cup finely chopped green pepper
¼ cup corn oil
2 tablespoons fresh lime juice
12 whole cloves
¼ teaspoon salt

Place the duck pieces into a nonmetallic container. Mix the rest of the ingredients, then pour over the duck pieces. Cover and marinate at room temperature for 1 hour, turning from time to time.

Build a hot charcoal fire and let it burn down to coals. Drain the duck pieces. Heat the marinade to a boil in a saucepan, then keep it warm for use as a baste. Grill the duck pieces for about 30 minutes, turning from time to time and basting with the reserved marinade. Serve with rice and grilled papaya, below, which should be grilled along with the duck.

Grilled Papaya

2 papayas
¼ cup melted butter
½ teaspoon salt
⅛ teaspoon freshly grated nutmeg

Peel, halve, and seed the papayas. Put the halves into a bowl. Mix the butter, nutmeg, and salt; pour over the papayas, turning to coat all sides. Grill the papaya halves over the coals until just heated through, turning once. Serve with duck.

Smoked Duck, Chinese-Style

In China, duck is more popular than chicken, and it is cooked in a variety of ways. Here's one of my favorite recipes, combining a light salt cure and a short but intense smoking period followed by a long, slow steaming. To smoke the duck Chinese-style, you'll need a large pot with a lid and some sort of rack to hold the bird just off the bottom. (Wire racks are available.) A large stove-top cast-iron Dutch oven will work. If you prefer, you can cold-smoke the duck for a longer period of time. After smoking the bird, you'll need a steamer. The smoking rig can also be used for steaming. Finally, the duck should be deep-fried. The Dutch oven can be used for this, also.

2 large wild ducks
½ cup rice (uncooked)
½ cup brown sugar
½ cup black tea leaves
orange peel
2 tablespoons salt
2 tablespoons Szechuan peppercorns, crushed
1 teaspoon sodium nitrate
water
peanut oil

Mix the brown sugar, salt, crushed peppercorns, and sodium nitrate. Rub the duck with this mixture inside and out, then hang it in a cool, airy place for 6 to 8 hours. When you are ready to smoke the bird, peel the orange and use a fillet knife to cut off the bitter white inner lining. Cut the peel into pieces. Combine the rice, orange peel, and tea in the Dutch oven. Rig a rack just off the bottom and arrange the duck pieces on it. Cover the Dutch oven tightly and cook on medium heat for 10 minutes. Reduce heat to low. Turn the duck and heat for another 10 minutes. Rig for steaming over boiling water. Steam the duck, breast side up, for 1½ hours. Add more water if needed.

After steaming, dry the duck and then deep-fry it in peanut oil. The oil should be very hot—at least 375 degrees, and preferably hotter. Fry only until the skin is crispy. Disjoint the bird and cut it into bite-size pieces suitable for eating with chopsticks.

Note: If you prefer, the deep-frying step can be omitted, since the steaming fully cooks the bird.

Big Grill Duck, Chinese-Style

This recipe works best with a large charcoal grill with a cover. Build the fire in one side, and cook the duck in the other.

> 2 large wild ducks
> 1 large onion, chopped
> 4 cloves garlic, chopped
> ½ cup peanut oil
> ½ cup sake or dry vermouth
> ¼ cup soy sauce
> juice of 1 large lemon
> 2 tablespoons brown sugar
> 1 tablespoon grated fresh ginger root

Disjoint the ducks and split the breast. Save the giblets and bony pieces for soup or stew. Mix the peanut oil, vermouth, soy sauce, lemon juice, brown sugar, onion, garlic, and ginger root. Put the duck pieces into a nonmetallic container, pour in the marinade mixture, toss to coat all sides, and refrigerate overnight. Drain the ducks, saving the marinade.

Build a charcoal fire in one side of a large covered-wagon type grill (or any large grill suitable for indirect cooking). When the coals are ready, place the duck pieces on the opposite side of the grill. Use wood chips for smoke if you like. Close the cover. In a saucepan, bring the reserved marinade to a light boil, reduce the heat, and simmer for 10 minutes. Baste the duck pieces with this mixture every 15 minutes or so. Cook until the pieces are medium rare, usually about 2 hours, depending on your fire and the grill. Do not overcook. If in doubt, cut into the thickest part of one of the thighs to check for doneness.

Easy Smoked Duck

Here's a recipe for use with large wild ducks and a silo-type cooker-smoker, complete with a water pan and wood chips.

> 4 large ducks, plucked and drawn
> thin-sliced bacon
> juice of 1 lemon
> salt and pepper

Build a fire in the smoker unit, fill the pan with water, and add some fresh green hardwood chips, or old chips that have been soaked in water. Rub the ducks inside and out with lemon juice, then sprinkle inside and out with salt and pepper. Wrap the birds with thin-sliced bacon, covering all surfaces, and secure the bacon with toothpicks. Place the ducks breast side up in the smoker. Smoke for 8 to 12 hours, adding more wood chips and water to the pan from time to time. The exact time will depend on the smoker, the heat, and the size of the birds, as well as other variables such as the outside temperature and the wind. Experience is the best guide, but even the expert will want to slice deep into a breast to make sure it is done before serving. The meat should be pink, but should not run blood. Serve whole for a main meal, allowing a duck for each person, or slice as appetizers.

A. D.'s Rotisserie Duck

This recipe can be used to grill 2 or 3 mallard-size or smaller ducks on a rotisserie.

> 2 or 3 mallards or smaller ducks
> 1 cup olive oil
> ½ cup red wine vinegar
> ¼ cup soy sauce
> ¼ cup chopped parsley
> 4 cloves garlic, crushed
> salt and pepper to taste

Build a charcoal fire in the grill and rig the rotisserie. Mix the oil, wine vinegar, soy sauce, parsley, garlic, salt, and pepper in a saucepan. Simmer for about 10 minutes. Keep warm. When the coals are hot, place the birds on the rotisserie, following the manufacturer's instructions. Grill until the birds are medium rare. (The cooking times will vary with the rig you are using, your fire, and the size of the birds. With most rigs, 1½ hours will be about right. If in doubt, cut into a bird before serving.) Baste several times while grilling.

Duck and Bacon on a Spit

Bacon wrapped around ducks to be cooked over open coals helps keep the meat from drying out. With the birds about 6 inches over a medium hot fire, the meat will be done when the bacon is ready to eat. These birds need no basting and can be either plucked or skinned, provided that they are well covered with bacon. I like thin bacon, which will allow for a little over-lapping. During the last few minutes of grilling, sprinkle with salt, pepper, and a little paprika. Also, I sometimes use a little lemon-pepper seasoning.

The biggest problem is caused by the grease dripping from the bacon, which can cause fires. If you are using a rotisserie or a spit in a fixed position (as in forked sticks on either side), put a drip pan of some sort directly under the spit. You can fashion one from heavy-duty aluminum foil.

Ducks cooked over a green wood fire will be partly smoked— to advantage. Also, fresh wood chips, or water-soaked chips, can be added to charcoal or wood fires.

Smoked Goose

This recipe, adapted from *Dress 'Em Out*, by Captain James A. Smith, can be used in most commercial or home-rigged smokers. The list of ingredients calls for saltpeter. I have substituted sodium nitrite, which is available at most pharmacy shops. Like sodium nitrate, it helps cure the meat and gives it a red color.

1 wild goose
⅔ cup salt
1 tablespoon sugar
1 teaspoon sodium nitrite
1 teaspoon freshly ground black pepper
1 clove garlic, peeled and split

Pluck the goose, wash it in cold water, and pat it dry. Thoroughly mix the salt, pepper, sugar, and sodium nitrite. Rub the goose inside and out with the garlic and salt mix. Place the goose in a crock or nonmetallic container (such as a plastic ice chest), and cover it with a cloth and a lid. Keep it in a cool place for 7 days, turning every day or so. Remove the goose, cover with a fresh cheesecloth (I souse mine with bacon drippings), and smoke at 200 degrees until done, which will take several hours. Chill the meat. Slice very thin before serving.

SEVEN

Broiled Ducks and Geese

Broiling is a method of cooking meats directly under a heat source, whereas grilling is accomplished directly over a heat source. With either method, the ideal is to cook the meat so that the outside is nicely browned and crispy at the same time that the inside is only medium rare. The general rule: The thinner the meat, the closer it can be cooked to the heat. Of course, the intensity of the heat can also be a factor, but most broiling these days is done under electric heating elements of fairly uniform output. Broiling can also be done under gas heat, but electric heat with adjustable racks works much better, at least for me. It follows that thin breast fillets can be broiled 2 or 3 inches from the heat for a short period of time, whereas whole birds should be 10 inches or so away for a longer period of time. Duck leg quarters and goose thighs usually work best at 5 or 6 inches.

If the meat is good, it's best to broil it with the skin on. The skin prevents the meat from drying out and gives a nice color to the cooked bird. If the skin is removed, try wrapping the meat with thin strips of bacon, which will provide basting oil, flavor, and, when cooked crisply, color.

Once you master the principle of broiling, recipes really aren't necessary, as you can easily come up with your own creations, such as sprinkling lightly with paprika and lemon-pepper seasoning salt. It's more fun that way, but here are a few recipes to get you started, if you need 'em.

Broiled Duck Halves

The keys to success with this recipe are to get the birds done without overcooking and to hold the basting sauce until the end. Using the sauce too early will result in a burnt surface before the inside gets done.

The Birds
4 to 6 duck halves
bacon drippings
salt

The Sauce
2 tablespoons butter
2 tablespoons brown sugar
juice of 1 lemon
1 tablespoon Worcestershire sauce
1 tablespoon catsup
2 cloves garlic, crushed

Pluck and draw the ducks, then split them in half lengthwise. Preheat the broiler. Salt the duck halves on both sides, then broil them 6 to 8 inches from the heat, basting frequently with bacon drippings. Mix the sauce ingredients together. When the duck halves are almost done, baste several times with the sauce. Serve a duck half on each plate, along with vegetables and hot bread.

Broiled Teal

Here's an old Creole recipe for whole teal or other small ducks. Note that the bird is cooked least 6 inches from the heat source and is turned frequently. Do not overcook.

6 teal
6 strips bacon
6 slices toast
melted butter
salt and pepper
lemon juice
chopped parsley
parsley sprigs (for garnish)
lemon slices (for garnish)
red currant jelly (for garnish)

Pluck the birds, draw, and rub inside and out with melted butter. Sprinkle with salt and pepper. Wrap each bird with a strip of bacon, fastened with a skewer, and broil about 6 inches from the heat source for about 30 minutes, turning frequently to prevent burning. Mix a little melted butter, lemon juice, and chopped parsley; spread this mixture over the breasts of the birds. Serve on toast, garnished with parsley, lemon slices, and red currant jelly. Serve hot.

Sylvia's Wild Goose Breast

This great recipe has been adapted from *The Bounty of the Earth Cookbook,* by Sylvia Bashline. Although I highly recommend the recipe, I do have a disagreement with the author. She says that the measures serve 4, which would allow each person only half a goose breast fillet. The dish is so good, however, that I'll want a whole fillet for myself.

The Bird
1 goose breast, skinned and filleted
½ cup red wine
½ cup soy sauce
¼ cup cooking oil
¼ teaspoon ground pepper

Mix the soy sauce, wine, oil, and pepper. Place the fillets in a nonmetallic container of suitable size, and pour the marinade mixture over them. Marinate for 2½ hours, turning from time to time. Preheat the broiler, adjusting the rack so that the fillets will be 5 inches under the heat. Drain the fillets, place them on a greased broiling pan, and broil them for 10 minutes on each side. Place the fillets on a wooden carving board and slice diagonally against the grain. Serve hot with the heated sauce, made as follows:

The Sauce
¼ cup black raspberry jelly
¼ cup water
1½ tablespoons Dijon-type mustard
1 teaspoon lime juice
1 teaspoon soy sauce
½ teaspoon steak sauce
¼ teaspoon ground caraway seeds
salt and pepper

Mix all the sauce ingredients in a saucepan, heat, and serve in a heated bowl or gravy boat. Spoon a little sauce over each slice of broiled goose breast.

Broiled Coot Breast

The measures in this recipe can be increased or reduced as needed. I allow at least one coot per person.

4 coots
½ cup lime or lemon juice
4 tablespoons soy sauce
4 tablespoons butter
4 or 5 slices fresh ginger root
1 tablespoon pepper
10 water chestnuts, sliced

Skin and breast the coots. Put the breasts into a pot, cover with water, and simmer for 1 to 2 hours, or until the breasts are very tender. Mix the lime juice, soy sauce, and pepper. Put the parboiled coot breasts into a nonmetallic bowl or Ziploc bag, add the marinade, toss to coat all sides, and marinate in the refrigerator for 3 or 4 hours. Preheat the broiler. Drain the marinade into a saucepan. Add the butter and ginger root. Bring to a boil, and remove from heat. Place the coot breasts on a greased rack and broil 3 or 4 inches from the heat for about 10 minutes, turning and basting several times. Top each breast with a layer of water chestnut slices and broil for a few more minutes. Serve hot.

EIGHT

Pies and Casseroles

Although not often cooked in America, duck pies and casseroles make very good eating, and they might well be the very best way to introduce nonhunters to the rich flavor of waterfowl. Thousands of recipes could be used in this chapter, but I have kept the number to a few of my favorites.

Teal Pie

For this dish you will need a double pie crust, top and bottom. Use your favorite pastry recipe and a deep pie pan, or purchase a double crust from the supermarket.

  2 or 3 teal or other small ducks
  1 large onion
  1 tablespoon chopped fresh parsley
  1 tablespoon Worcestershire sauce
  2 chicken bouillon cubes
  diced potatoes
  diced carrots
  green peas
  sliced mushrooms (optional)
  diced red bell pepper (optional)
  pie pastry
  Kitchen Bouquet
  salt and pepper
  water

Put the ducks into a suitable pot and cover with water. Add the bouillon cubes, Worcestershire sauce, chopped onion, parsley, salt, and pepper. Bring to a boil, reduce the heat to low, cover, and simmer for 1 hour or so, until the ducks are tender. Drain the ducks, cool, bone, and dice the meat. Boil the pot liquid until it is reduced by half. Add the Kitchen Bouquet to taste—a level teaspoonful is about right for me. Stir and cook a little longer, until you have a gravy. (Add a little cornstarch if you are in a hurry.)

Preheat the oven to 450 degrees. Place the diced duck into the pie shell. Top with diced potatoes, diced carrots, peas, and if you like, sliced mushrooms. Sprinkle on a little diced red bell pepper, if available. Cover with gravy. Top with pie pastry. Bake in the center of the oven for 15 minutes, then reduce the oven temperature to 350 and bake for another 20 minutes, or until the pie is nicely browned.

Easy Variation: Use frozen mixed vegetables or frozen soup vegetables to fill the pie pan. I sprinkle these over the duck and allow them to thaw or soften somewhat before pouring in the gravy. Some of the frozen soup mixes now have tomato, which adds a nice touch of color to the pie.

Easy Duck Pie

Here's an easy pie that can be made with fresh, frozen, or canned mixed green peas and carrots.

> 1 large wild duck or equivalent
> 2 cups mixed peas and carrots
> 1 can cream of mushroom soup (10¾-ounce size)
> 2 medium onions, chopped
> 1 cup milk
> ½ cup flour
> 1 stick butter or margarine, frozen
> salt and pepper
> water
> 2 or 3 bay leaves

Dress and disjoint the duck. Place the pieces in a pot along with some salt, pepper, bay leaves, about half of the onions, and enough water to cover everything. Bring to a boil, reduce the heat, and simmer for 1 hour or longer, until the meat is tender. Remove the bird and save the pot broth. While waiting for the bird to cool a little, preheat the oven to 450 degrees. Bone the bird, placing the meat into a casserole dish. Add the peas and carrots, the rest of the onions, mushroom soup, and about ½ cup of the broth. Mix the milk and flour, then pour the mixture over the vegetables. Grate the frozen butter evenly over everything. Bake for about 30 minutes, or until the top is nicely browned. Feeds 2 to 4.

A. D.'s Duck Pie

This dish is best cooked in a Dutch oven that can be heated on top of the stove, then transferred to an oven. To prepare the meat, breast 4 ducks, fillet each breast, and cut each fillet in half across the grain, making 16 chunks of meat.

>8 duck breast fillets, halved
>8 slices bacon
>4 medium potatoes, diced
>4 carrots, sliced
>8 green onions with part of tops, cut into
>1-inch segments
>2 hard-boiled chicken eggs, chopped
>1 cup sherry
>pie pastry or refrigerated biscuit dough
>2 bay leaves
>salt and pepper
>water

Fry the bacon in a Dutch oven. Drain. In the bacon drippings, brown the duck pieces all around. Sprinkle with salt and pepper. Crumble the bacon and add it to the pot. Cover with water, add the bay leaves, and bring to a boil. Cover tightly, reduce the heat to low, and simmer for 1 hour. Add the carrots, potatoes, and gren onions, along with the sherry and enough water to almost cover the vegetables and meat, but not quite. Cover and simmer for 30 minutes. Fold in the chopped eggs.

Preheat the oven to 400 degrees. Make a batch of pastry by a recipe of your choice, or pop open a can of refrigerated biscuits and mix them up. Sprinkle some flour on a flat surface and roll the dough flat. Cut the pastry into strips about ½ inch wide and crisscross them on top of the duck and vegetable mixture. Place the Dutch oven in the preheated oven and bake, uncovered, for 20 minutes, or until the pastry is browned. Feeds 4.

Duck Casserole Supreme

Here's a super duck casserole, adapted from Duck Unlimited's *After the Hunt Cookbook,* to which it was submitted by Sherry Tanner of Russellville, Arkansas. The recipe called for 1 package of wild and long-grain rice, without listing a size. I use Uncle Ben's, cooked by the directions on the package. I also use the giblets when I cook this recipe, but suit yourself. The original recipe called for a 6-ounce can of sliced mushrooms. I have specified 8 ounces fresh edible mushrooms, which are widely available these days in supermarkets and in the wild.

    2 mallard-size ducks or equivalent
    2 ribs celery with tops, chopped
    1 medium onion, sliced
    1 medium onion, chopped
    8 ounces fresh edible mushrooms
    1 package wild and long-grain rice (7- or 8-ounce size)
    1½ cups milk
    ½ cup butter
    ¼ cup flour
    1 tablespoon chopped fresh parsley
    1 package slivered almonds (2-ounce size)
    salt and pepper
    water

Dress and disjoint the birds. Put the pieces and giblets into a pot, along with the sliced onion and chopped celery. Cover with water and bring to a boil. Then cover tightly, reduce the heat, and simmer for 2 hours. Cook the rice by the directions on the package. Preheat the oven. Bone and chop the duck meat into small, bite-size pieces. In a large skillet, sauté the chopped onion in butter. Stir in the flour. Add the mushrooms, milk, parsley, salt, and pepper, mixing well. Mix in the cooked rice and duck pieces. Turn into a well-greased 2-quart casserole dish. Sprinkle with almonds, then bake for 25 minutes. Feeds 4.

Duck Normandy

Here's a very rich dish that makes excellent use of cooking apples, brandy, and butter. Use real butter in this one.

> 3 large wild ducks
> 6 medium apples
> 6 tablespoons butter (divided)
> ½ cup brandy
> salt and pepper

Pluck and disjoint the ducks, cutting them into breast and leg quarters. (Save the bony pieces and giblets for another recipe.) Heat 3 tablespoons of butter in a large skillet. Sprinkle the duck pieces with salt and pepper, brown them in hot butter, and set aside to drain. Peel, core, and slice the apples. Heat the rest of the butter in the skillet, then cook the apples for a few minutes. Preheat the oven to 350 degrees. Place some of the apples in a layer in the bottom of a buttered casserole dish. Place the duck pieces atop the apples. Surround and top the duck pieces with the rest of the apples. To the drippings in the skillet, add ½ cup of brandy. Heat and stir with a wooden spoon, loosening any particles from the bottom of the skillet. Pour the heated brandy over the duck and apples. Cover and bake for 1½ hours. Serve hot in the casserole dish. Feeds 4 to 6.

Easy Duck Breast Casserole

Here's a delicious dish, easy to prepare, that I like to cook with wild duck breasts, saving the rest of the birds for soup.

> 8 duck breast fillets (from 4 large wild ducks)
> 1 can celery soup (10¾-ounce size)
> ½ soup can water
> 8 ounces sliced wild mushrooms
> 1 cup cream sherry
> salt and freshly ground black pepper

Preheat the oven to 350 degrees. Place the duck breasts into a greased casserole dish. Cover with sliced mushrooms, salt, and pepper. Mix the soup, water, and sherry. Pour evenly over the casserole. Cover and cook for 1½ hours. Remove the dish, uncover, and cut the breasts across the grain into ½-inch slices. Return to the casserole dish and bake, uncovered, for 40 minutes, stirring a time or two. Serve hot, along with the gravy, rice or noodles, vegetables, and bread. Feeds 3 to 6. Can be stretched with lots of rice.

Mexican Duck Casserole

Although the wild duck, along with the turkey, was domesticated in Mexico long before the Europeans brought over chickens, old recipes are hard to come by. Here's a good one, making use of a great American vegetable (or fruit)—the tomato—and some European ingredients brought here by the Spanish. Most of the Mexican recipes that call for tomatoes say to peel and seed them, but I seldom go that far. Suit yourself.

3 mallards
2 large tomatoes, chopped
1 large onion, chopped
3 cloves garlic, minced
½ cup chopped fresh cilantro (with roots if available)
¼ cup seedless raisins
¼ cup dry sherry
¼ cup orange juice
¼ cup slivered almonds, toasted
2 bay leaves
½ teaspoon chopped fresh thyme
¼ teaspoon chopped fresh oregano
salt and pepper
butter
flour

Pluck and draw the ducks, and cut them into quarters. (Save the bony parts and giblets for other purposes.) Sprinkle the pieces with salt and pepper, shake them in flour, and brown them, a few pieces at a time, in a skillet with some butter. As they brown, arrange the duck pieces in a large casserole dish that has a cover. Preheat the oven to 325 degrees. Add the tomatoes, onion, garlic, cilantro, raisins, almonds, bay leaves, thyme, oregano, salt, pepper, and orange juice. Cover and bake for 1 hour, or until the duck is tender. Place the duck pieces on a heated serving platter. If the birds were very fat, skim the pan drippings. Transfer the drippings to a saucepan. Mix in the sherry. Mix ½ tablespoon flour with a little melted butter or fat, then stir it into the sauce. Cook for several minutes, stirring as you go. Serve the ducks on the platter and the gravy separately, along with rice, vegetables, and salad. Feeds 4 to 6.

Outer Banks Casserole

This recipe is from coastal Carolina, historically a hot spot for ducks and geese. The ingredients list calls for wild rice mix. There are several of these on the market, such as Uncle Ben's, and they should be cooked by the directions on the package.

> 2 or 3 large wild ducks
> 1 package wild and long-grain rice
>   (7- or 8-ounce size)
> 3 ribs celery with tops, chopped
> 1 large onion, quartered
> 1 medium onion, chopped
> 8 ounces fresh mushrooms, sliced
> 2 hard-boiled chicken eggs, chopped
> 1½ cups half and half
> ½ cup butter
> ½ cup slivered almonds
> ¼ cup flour
> 2 bay leaves
> 1 tablespoon chopped fresh parsley
> salt and pepper

Quarter the ducks, saving the giblets. Put the duck pieces and giblets into a large pot. Barely cover with water. Stir in the celery, onion quarters, and bay leaves, along with a little salt and pepper. Bring to a boil, then reduce the heat, cover, and simmer for 1 hour, or until the ducks are tender. Remove the duck pieces, bone, and chop the meat into bite-size pieces. Strain and save the stock, discarding the celery, onion, and bay leaves. While the duck simmers, cook the rice according to the directions on the package. Melt the butter in a large skillet, then sauté the chopped onion and mushrooms for 5 minutes or so. Cut the ducks into serving pieces and dress out the giblets and bony pieces. Preheat the oven to 350 degrees. Add 1½ cups of the reserved duck broth to the skillet, then stir in the flour. Simmer until the mixture thickens a little. Add the duck pieces and chopped giblets, cooked rice, half and half, parsley, and chopped chicken eggs. Spoon the mixture into a greased 2-quart casserole dish suitable for serving. Sprinkle the top with slivered almonds. Cover and bake for 20 minutes. Remove the lid and bake for a few more minutes. Feeds 4. Serve with fresh peas and other vegetables, along with hot biscuits.

R. C.'s Favorite

R. C. Gormley, who lives part of the year in Maryland and part in Montana, tells me that his favorite goose recipe is the way his wife cooks it, as follows. A sort of casserole, it can be prepared ahead of time and reheated or frozen for a future meal. I have adapted the recipe (adding some salt and pepper) from a book called *Cookin' on the Wild Side*, published by the Grand National Waterfowl Association.

> 1 wild goose, plucked and drawn
> 1 large onion, chunked
> 1 carrot, chunked
> 1 can cream of celery soup (10 3/4-ounce size)
> 1 small can water chestnuts, sliced (8-ounce size)
> 4 tablespoons red currant jelly
> salt and pepper (optional)
> water

Preheat the oven to 375 degrees. Place the goose in a roasting pan. Add ½ cup water, along with the carrots and onions. Cover tightly and cook for 1 hour. Cool, skin, and slice the goose meat, placing it in a casserole dish. Mix a sauce with the soup, currant jelly, and water chestnuts. Add salt and pepper, if desired. Spread the sauce over the sliced goose. Heat up in the oven and serve hot.

NINE

Soups, Stews, and Gumbos

Since duck soup is so easy to make, many cooks will come up with their own recipes, using available vegetables along with barley and other soup ingredients. Although I enjoy an ongoing adventure with duck soup, other cooks may feel a need to proceed in a more organized manner, using recipes that can be repeated from time to time. I hope this chapter will help.

A true gumbo is a little more complicated than soups, and the typical list of ingredients tends to be rather long. Although the word *gumbo* comes from an African word meaning okra, many modern recipes called gumbo omit this ingredient. This is a culinary sin. Okra imparts a mucilaginous texture that is essential to the real stuff. It's best to use young, tender pods of fresh or frozen okra, sliced into ¾-inch wheels.

A similar quality can be obtained by the judicious use of filé, which is made from pulverized dried sassafras leaves. If you can't pick and dry your own, you can purchase filé in most spice markets. Be careful with this stuff. If you add too much to very hot gumbo, you'll have a stringy mess. Actually, it's best to use the filé in individual servings. That way, you keep it out of the main pot. The trick is to ladle the gumbo into bowls, stir in filé to taste, and add a dollop of rice last.

Easy Goose or Duck Gumbo

The list of ingredients calls for 3 cups of diced duck or goose meat. The exact amount isn't critical, so use more or less, depending on what you've got on hand. I usually use meat from legs and thighs, saving the breast for other recipes. It's best to have chunks of meat, no smaller than 1 inch. The ingredients list also calls for frozen gumbo vegetables, a commercially available mix that contains quite a bit of okra. Okra is essential to the texture, so don't be tempted to substitute a frozen soup or stew blend.

> 3 cups goose or duck meat, cut in bite-size chunks
> ½ pound smoked venison sausage
> 3 cups chicken broth or duck stock
> 1 can tomatoes (16-ounce size)
> 1 package frozen gumbo vegetable mix
>   (16-ounce size)
> 1 medium onion, diced
> 1 rib celery with leaves
> 3 cloves garlic
> 2 tablespoons fresh parsley
> 1 teaspoon salt
> ½ teaspoon pepper
> 2 bay leaves
> rice (cooked separately)

Cut the sausage into ¾-inch wheels and brown them in a stove-top Dutch oven. Add the tomatoes (chopped), juice from the tomatoes, and frozen gumbo vegetables. Turn to high heat. Peel the onion and dice it. Peel the garlic and mince it. Scrape the celery if it is tough and dice it finely, along with the green tops. Put the onions, garlic, celery, parsley, bay leaves, salt, and pepper into the pot. Bring to a boil, then reduce the heat, cover, and simmer for 1 hour. Add the goose meat, cover, and simmer for another hour. Serve hot in bowls, along with rice and plenty of hot French bread.

Note: For this recipe, it is permissible to put the rice into a bowl, then add the gumbo. In a filé recipe, the process should be reversed.

Duck and Venison Sausage Filé Gumbo

Here's a combination that the hunter often has available. I prefer to use a relatively dry, smoked venison sausage made without much fat. The ingredients list specifies large wild ducks, but you can substitute 3 to 5 smaller ducks. The exact amount isn't critical.

2 large wild ducks
1 pound smoked venison sausage in ¾-inch slices
⅓ cup peanut oil
½ cup flour
2 medium onions, chopped
1 red bell pepper, chopped
¼ cup chopped fresh parsley
4 cloves garlic, minced
1 tablespoon salt
1 teaspoon crushed dried thyme
1 teaspoon black pepper
½ teaspoon red pepper flakes
3 bay leaves
filé powder
water

Skin, draw, and disjoint the ducks. Cut the breasts in half lengthwise, then cut the leg quarters into thighs and drumsticks. Dress the gizzard. Put the bony parts and giblets into a pot, cover with water, and add the bay leaves and red pepper flakes. Bring to a boil, reduce the heat, cover, and simmer until the duck meat is very tender. Bone the pieces, setting the meat aside. Discard the bay leaves, then measure the liquid in the pot. Add to it or subtract from it enough water to make 2 quarts. Put the water and the boned duck back into the pot, bring to heat, and simmer.

Heat the oil in a skillet. Brown the duck pieces, then put them into the simmering pot. Also brown the sausage pieces, adding them to the pot. Slowly stir the flour into the oil left in the skillet. (You should have about ½ cup of oil left, depending on how much the sausage and duck pieces soaked up. If you were working with very fatty sausage, you may have too much oil. Measure it if unsure, adding more or reducing as needed.) Heat the flour and oil mixture, stirring with a wooden spoon, until you have a brown roux; 30 minutes of cooking and stirring isn't too long, if you have the time and the elbow grease. Add the onion, red bell pepper, garlic, and parsley. Sauté for 5 minutes. Add ½ cup of the duck broth, along with the salt, black pepper, and thyme. Pour the contents of the skillet into the pot, using your wooden spoon to get all the gravy. Stir the pot, bring to a light boil, reduce the heat, cover, and simmer for 2 hours.

Serve hot. Ladle the gumbo into individual bowls, then carefully stir in a little filé to taste. Add the rice last. Have ready plenty of hot French bread. Feast.

Goose Gumbo with Oysters

Although a true gumbo is made with the aid of okra, or is at least helped along at the end with a pinch of filé, I won't argue the point if a good roux binds the flavors and some fresh oysters are added to the ingredients.

> 1 wild goose
> 1 pint freshly shucked oysters
> 3 medium onions, chopped
> 3 cloves garlic, chopped
> ½ green bell pepper, chopped
> ½ red bell pepper, chopped
> ½ cup fresh chives or green onion tops, chopped
> ½ cup celery with leaves, chopped
> ½ cup bacon drippings
> ½ cup flour
> ½ teaspoon red pepper flakes
> salt and black pepper to taste
> water
> 2 bay leaves
> rice (cooked separately)

Shuck out a pint of oysters, saving and straining the liquid from the shells. Skin and disjoint the goose. Cut the breast in half, then separate the drumsticks and thighs. Save the liver, heart, and gizzard from the innards. The gizzard should be cut in half, turned inside out, and skinned. Put the bony pieces (wings, back, and neck) into a pot, then add the bay leaves, and red pepper flakes. Cover with water. Bring to a boil, then reduce the heat, cover, and simmer for 2 hours, or until the meat tends to fall from the bones. Pull the meat from the bony pieces, put it back into the pot, and discard the bones, along with the bay leaves. Measure the liquid and retain it.

In a cast-iron pot, large skillet, or stove-top Dutch oven, heat the bacon drippings, slowly stir in the flour, and continue to cook and stir constantly with a wooden spoon until you have a dark brown roux. Take 30 minutes to make the roux, if you've got the time. Fanatics might insist on even longer stirring. After the roux browns, add the onions, bell peppers, celery, garlic, and chives or green onion tops. Cook for 5 minutes. Add the chopped boiled goose meat. Measure the liquid from the pot, and add to it the oyster liquor and enough water to make 3 quarts. Add the liquid to the Dutch oven, along with the goose pieces, salt, and pepper. Bring to a boil, reduce the heat, and simmer (do not boil) for 2 hours. Add the oysters. Simmer for 5 or 6 minutes, then remove from the heat. Serve the gumbo in bowls with rice.

Teal and Venison Sausage Gumbo

Any good smoked link sausage can be used with this recipe, but I prefer a low-fat venison sausage. The Cajun andouille sausage is also very good. When you shuck the oysters, be sure to strain and save the liquor. When dressing the teal, cut them into quarters, halving the breasts.

3 teal, quartered
2 pounds smoked sausage, cut into pieces
½ pint freshly shucked oysters
1 cup oyster liquor
½ cup lard or shortening
1 cup sliced fresh okra
2 medium onions, chopped
1 turnip root, peeled and chopped
½ green bell pepper, chopped
½ red bell pepper, chopped
3 cloves garlic, minced
¼ cup chopped fresh parsley
2 tablespoons Worcestershire sauce
2 bay leaves
salt and pepper
flour
hot water
rice (cooked separately)

Heat the lard in a stove-top Dutch oven. Brown and drain the duck quarters. Stir the flour into the lard. Cook on low, stirring constantly with a wooden spoon—the longer the better, within reason—until the roux is dark brown. Thirty minutes cooking and stirring on very low heat isn't too long, especially if you are using a cast-iron Dutch oven, as well you should be.

Add the onions, bell peppers, okra, and garlic. Cook for about 5 minutes. Warm the oyster liquor in a saucepan, then stir it into the Dutch oven mixture. Add the browned duck pieces, along with enough hot water to cover everything. Bring to a light boil, then reduce the heat. Stir in the salt, pepper, Worcestershire sauce, parsley, bay leaves, and chopped turnip. Cover and simmer for 1 hour. In a skillet, brown the sausage pieces, then add them to the pot, cover, and simmer for 30 minutes. Add the oysters and simmer for 20 minutes. While the gumbo is still very hot, ladle some into individual serving bowls along with some rice. Enjoy.

Stewed Duck with Rice

Here's one of my favorite dishes, which I also cook with the breast of dove, snipe, or other birds with dark meat. For this recipe, I like to use 1 mallard or 2 smaller ducks. Normally, I use only the breast and giblets, saving the bony parts for other dishes.

> breast fillets and giblets from 1 mallard or 2 teal
> ¼ pound smoked sausage, cut into bite-size pieces
> 2 tomatoes
> 1 medium-to-large onion, chopped
> 1 cup rice
> 1 tablespoon chopped fresh parsley (optional)
> 2 bay leaves
> salt and red pepper flakes to taste

Cut the breast into bite-size pieces. Clean the gizzard, turning it inside out, and cut it into 3 pieces. Put the breast and gizzard pieces into a pot or stove-top Dutch oven, cover with water, add the bay leaves, and simmer for 1 hour. Add the sausage, chopped onions, salt, red pepper flakes, and a little hot water if needed. Cut the liver into bite-size pieces, then add them to the pot. Simmer for 30 minutes. Discard the bay leaves. Bring to a new boil, then add the rice, parsley, and chopped tomato. Cook for 25 minutes, adding more water as needed. Serve hot in bowls.

Old Duck Stew with Easy Dumplings

Here's an ideal way to cook tough old ducks. The ingredients list calls for refrigerated tortillas to be used for easy dumplings. If you have a favorite recipe for tortillas, use it if you are so inclined. If you use the refrigerated kind, both flour and cornmeal tortillas are good. Why not try a mixture of both?

2 ducks
3 medium-to-large onions, cut into quarters
3 medium-to-large carrots, cut into pieces
8 ounces fresh mushrooms
2 hard-boiled chicken eggs, sliced
flour or corn tortillas
flour
water
½ teaspoon red pepper flakes
salt

Pluck or skin the ducks, depending on their quality, and cut them in half lengthwise. Place the birds into a stove-top Dutch oven, then put the onions, carrots, and mushrooms on top. Add the salt and red pepper flakes, and barely cover with water. Bring to a boil, then reduce the heat to very low, cover tightly, and simmer for 2 hours, adding a little water from time to time if needed. Remove the bird halves, placing them on a heated platter. Make a paste with a little flour and water, then stir it slowly into the pot liquid to thicken it a little. Cut the tortillas into strips about ½ inch wide. Roll the strips and drop them into the pot. Simmer for a few minutes, then add the sliced egg. Using a ladle, put some of the gravy over the ducks, then put the vegetables and dumplings around the sides. If you've got some spicy pickled peaches or crab apples, add a few of them to the dish.

Easy Duck and Vegetable Soup

I like to make a soup with duck parts and a package of frozen mixed soup vegetables from the supermarket. These packages are very convenient and produce no surplus or waste. Normally, I add a stalk or two of celery, an onion, and possibly some mushrooms if I have them on hand, but an acceptable soup can be made with only the frozen vegetables and the duck, along with a little salt and pepper. For duck, I like to use the frame, neck, wings, and giblets from two mallards or from several smaller ducks—in other words, all the duck except the breast and leg quarters. A whole mallard-size bird can also be used to advantage.

duck parts (see comments above)
1 package frozen soup vegetables (16-ounce size)
1 medium onion, chopped
1 or 2 ribs celery with tops, chopped
8 ounces fresh mushrooms (optional)
½ cup long-grain rice (uncooked)
2 bay leaves
salt and pepper
water

Put the duck parts into a pot and add 4 cups of water and the bay leaves. Bring to a boil, then reduce the heat, cover tightly, and simmer for 1½ to 2 hours, or until the duck is tender. Remove the duck pieces and drain. To the stock in the pot, add the onions, celery, mushrooms, frozen vegetables, salt, and pepper. Turn heat to high and bring to a new boil while you pull the meat from the duck bones and chop it coarsely. Put the chopped meat back into the pot, add the rice, bring to a boil, reduce heat, cover tightly, and simmer for 25 minutes. Add a little more water if needed. Serve hot in soup bowls with plenty of hot French bread on the side. This soup makes a complete meal and really hits the spot on a cold day.

A. D.'s Duck Soup, Crock-Pot-Style

I used to cook a dish or two for Choctawhatchee Lodge, and my duck soup with lots of barley was a favorite. I also like to use lots of celery with the green tops. For the measures below, the exact amount of duck meat isn't critical, but two mallards are about right. This recipe was also used in my *Complete Fish & Game Cookbook*.

2 wild ducks, mallard-size
4 cups water
½ cup red wine
1 cup pearl barley
3 large ribs celery with tops, finely chopped
1 medium onion, chopped
3 cloves garlic, minced
1 tablespoon chopped chives
½ teaspoon pepper
salt
3 bay leaves

Skin the ducks. Fillet out each side of the breasts and set aside. Disjoint the rest of the ducks, put the pieces into a stove-top pot, and cover with water. Add the bay leaves, cover, and simmer slowly for 1 hour, or until the meat is tender. While the bony pieces simmer, cut the breast pieces into chunks and put them into the Crock-Pot. Add 4 cups water, salt, pepper, chives, celery, onion, and garlic. (It's best to scrape the stalks of celery, then cut the stalks into several strips lengthwise before chopping, making smaller-than-usual pieces.) Turn the Crock-Pot to low.

When the duck in the pot is tender, take it out and bone the meat. Chop the meat and giblets, adding them to the Crock-Pot. Add 2 cups of the duck broth and discard the rest. Stir in the pearl barley. Add the red wine. Cover and heat on low for 6 to 7 hours. Serve in bowls and eat hot with a good bread.

Warning: Make sure that you don't add more than 1 cup of pearl barley. This stuff soaks up lots of water and expands greatly. It may even push the top off the Crock-Pot. After the barley has cooked for an hour or so, remember to check the liquid in the pot. Add a little very hot water if needed.

Chunky Duck Stew

Here's a recipe for cooking a good, thick, basic stew from chunks
of duck meat.

> 4 ducks, mallard-size
> 4 medium onions, quartered
> 1 medium red bell pepper, seeded and cut into chunks
> 1 medium green bell pepper, seeded and cut into chunks
> 12 ounces fresh whole mushrooms, golf-ball size
> 4 cloves garlic, chopped
> 2 tablespoons flour
> ½ cup wine
> water
> cooking oil
> salt and pepper

Skin the ducks. Fillet the breasts, cutting each side into 3 or
4 pieces. Disjoint and bone the legs and thighs. Save the giblets
and bony parts for another recipe.

Heat a little oil in a skillet. Stir-fry the duck pieces for a few
minutes on high heat. Drain. Sauté the onions until they brown
nicely, perhaps burning a little in spots to bring out the full flavor. Add the mushrooms, garlic, bell peppers, duck meat, salt,
and pepper. Cover with water. Add the wine. Simmer, covered,
for 30 minutes. Mix the flour with a little hot water, then stir the
paste into the stew to thicken it.

Serve hot with vegetables and rice or egg noodles. Feeds
4 to 6.

Teal and Mushroom Stew

I like to cook this dish whenever I get a batch of edible wild mushrooms and small ducks, such as teal. I have also cooked it with a combination of doves and teal. Of course, the dish can also be cooked with other ducks in reduced numbers. This dish can also be cooked in camp, especially if you've got ducks and edible wild mushrooms handy.

> 6 teal, quartered
> 10 slices bacon
> 1 pound fresh mushrooms, sliced
> 1 large onion, chopped
> ¼ cup flour
> salt and pepper
> water

In a stove-top Dutch oven, fry the bacon until crisp. Remove, crumble, and set aside. Quickly brown the duck pieces in the bacon drippings. Drain and set aside. Using a wooden spoon, stir the flour a little at a time into the bacon drippings. Reduce heat and simmer until the flour browns, stirring all the while. Stir in enough water to make a thin gravy. Add the browned duck pieces, mushrooms, onion, crumbled bacon, salt, and pepper. Cover and simmer (do not boil) on low heat for at least 1 hour, or until the duck pieces are tender, depending partly on how hungry you are, stirring from time to time and adding a little water as needed. Serve over rice.

Variation: Add a cup of red wine if you have some on hand.

Judy Marsh's Coot Stew

I have adapted this recipe from a nice little book called *The Maine Way,* put together by Judy Marsh and Carole Dyer and first published by the Maine Department of Inland Fisheries and Wildlife back in 1978. Most of the recipes are credited to various people in various parts of Maine.

> several coots
> 1 quart water
> 1 quart tomatoes
> ¼ pound butter
> 5 egg-size onions
> 5 carrots, cut into chunks
> 3 tablespoons cider vinegar
> 3 tablespoons wine
> 2 to 4 beef bouillon cubes
> 1 large bay leaf
> 1 heaping teaspoon parsley
> ⅛ teaspoon marjoram
> salt and pepper
> flour

Put all the ingredients except the coots, butter, and flour into a large pot. Bring to a boil, cover, and simmer. As the pot heats up, breast the coots, cutting the meat (skinless now) into bite-size pieces. Shake the coot pieces in a bag with some flour, then brown them in butter in a skillet. Add the browned coot to the pot, then add a little water to the skillet to make a gravy. Tilt the skillet, pouring the gravy into the pot. Cover the pot, reduce the heat to very low, and simmer for at least 2 hours.

Note: Judy Marsh points out that almost any other meat can be substituted for the coot. Try any sea ducks. If you are still worried about the edibility of coots or sea ducks, be sure to skin them and trim off any fat. Also, marinate them in a solution of water and baking soda. (See chapter 11 for marinades.)

Chinese Duck Soup

As noted earlier in this book, the Chinese eat more ducks than chickens, and, of course, they have developed many distinguished recipes. I am especially fond of this soup, which depends in part on dried black mushrooms. These can be purchased in Chinese markets. Although they seem expensive, they expand after being soaked in water and have an intense flavor, so a few go a long way. This recipe is usually cooked with leftover meat from a large duck, but a small wild duck, such as a teal, can be simmered to provide the cooked meat. I have adapted the recipe from *The World Atlas of Food,* and in my version I use a teal to provide both the meat and the stock. You can also use the legs, thighs, and bony parts of 2 or 3 small ducks, saving the breasts for stir-fry.

> 1 teal or small wild duck, or 1 cup cooked duck meat
> ¾ cup freshly shelled green peas
> 4 medium-size dried Chinese black mushrooms
> 1 carrot, chopped
> 1 rib celery with tops, chopped
> 1 large onion, chopped
> 4 tablespoons white wine
> 2 tablespoons soy sauce
> cornstarch paste (see below)
> 1 large slice white bread
> peanut oil
> salt and freshly ground pepper

Soak the dried mushrooms in water for at least 30 minutes, then drain, trim, and mince them. Dress the duck and simmer it in water until tender, along with the chopped carrot, onion, and celery. Remove the duck and set aside to cool. Strain and save the stock. Pull all the meat from the duck and set it aside.

Heat 2½ cups of the stock in a boiler. (If you don't have 2½ cups of duck stock, add a little water to make up the difference.) Add the duck meat, mushrooms, and shelled peas. Simmer for

5 minutes. Stir 1 tablespoon of cornstarch into 3 tablespoons of water to make a paste. Stir this paste into the soup makings, along with the soy sauce, white wine, salt, and pepper. Bring to a simmer—not a boil—and cook until the soup thickens, stirring constantly. Remove the pan from the heat, but keep the soup hot.

Trim the bread and cut it into ½-inch cubes. Heat the oil until it is quite hot, then fry the bread cubes for a minute or two, until crisp and golden. Drain them on a brown bag. Put the hot soup into a tureen, then add the bread cubes. Serve hot.

Czarnina

Here's an unusual sweet-and-sour soup that can be cooked with a large wild goose or several ducks. You'll need 2 cups of blood from the birds, so be sure to take care of this as soon as the birds are dropped, while they are still warm. Czarnina is a Polish dish, and this version has been adapted from Walter Oleksy's *The Old Country Cookbook*.

> goose giblets
> 3 pounds pork neck bones or backbones
> 2 cups goose blood
> 2 cups prune juice
> 2 cups prunes
> 1 cup raisins
> 2 carrots, cut into chunks
> 1 onion, quartered lengthwise
> 3 tablespoons flour
> 2 tablespoons sugar
> vinegar to taste
> salt and pepper
> 6 quarts water
> noodles, cooked separately

Dress the gizzard. Place the pork neck bones and all of the giblets into a large stove-top Dutch oven or a suitable pot. Add the carrots, onions, salt, and pepper. Pour in the water. Bring to a boil, then reduce the heat to a simmer, cover tightly, and cook on very low heat for 1½ to 2 hours. Remove the pork and giblets. Strain the broth, returning it to the pot. Bone and chop the meat, adding it back to the broth. Simmer. Add the prunes, raisins, and prune juice. In a saucepan, heat the blood. Add about 1 tablespoon of vinegar. Stir in the sugar and flour, mixing until smooth. Slowly stir the blood mixture into the soup. Cover and simmer for 30 minutes, stirring from time to time. Taste. Czarnina should be sweet-and-sour. Add more vinegar or more sugar, if needed. Serve with cooked noodles.

Also see the Duck Giblet Soup recipe in chapter 10.

Duck and Goose Stock

Anytime you've got bony pieces of ducks or geese left over, don't throw them out. Use a recipe that calls for these parts, or make a stock that can be used as a base for soups or as an ingredient in other recipes. I don't hesitate to use duck stock in any recipe that calls for beef stock.

> bony parts
> water
> onion, chopped (optional)
> celery with tops, chopped (optional)
> carrots, chopped (optional)
> 2 bay leaves (optional)

Put the bony parts into a pot, add the bay leaves and chopped vegetables, if desired, and barely cover with water. Bring to a boil, cover, reduce the heat, and simmer for 2 to 3 hours. Strain the stock. It can be kept in the refrigerator for several days or frozen.

TEN

Giblets and Appetizers

The giblets of ducks and geese—liver, heart, and gizzard—can make very good eating and are often used in appetizers. These parts should be removed from the bird during field dressing and should be stored in a cool place, preferably on ice. I often use a plastic Ziploc bag for convenience.

When removing the liver from the rest of the innards, be careful not to puncture the gallbladder; it contains a bitter liquid that can discolor and impart a bad taste to the liver and the rest of the meat. When removing the gallbladder, it's best to slice off a little of the liver with it to avoid cutting into it.

To dress the gizzard, hold it flat and thinly slice into it, making a shallow cut about halfway around it. Then turn the gizzard, dumping out the contents, and peel off or scrape the inner lining.

When cooking the giblets, remember that the gizzard is on the tough side and requires long simmering. The heart should also be simmered for a long time, although it is not as tough as the gizzard. The liver is quite tender and cooks in a few minutes. In recipes where all the giblets are used together, it may be best to add the liver during the last 20 or 30 minutes.

In addition to giblet dishes and snacks, other parts of the duck can also be used for appetizers or finger food. A few suggestions, such as duck jerky, are included in this chapter.

Liver with Bacon

Duck or goose liver is very good when wrapped in bacon and broiled or grilled. If you've got large livers, cut them into bite-size pieces, wrap with half a strip of thin bacon, pin with a toothpick, and broil or grill for about 10 minutes, or until the bacon is ready to eat. Sprinkle with onion salt, then serve as an appetizer, or perhaps as a side dish with a duck or goose supper.

If you need more liver, mix in some liver from chicken, turtle, freshly caught fish, rabbit, or squirrel.

Variation: Sprinkle the liver with salt, dust with fine stone-ground white cornmeal, and wrap with bacon. Deep-fry until the bacon is done, then sprinkle lightly with Chinese five-spice powder (available in supermarkets) or very lightly with a little powdered cinnamon, and serve hot.

Sautéed Goose Livers

Here's a dish that I like to cook for myself, using 2 or more goose livers or a mixture of goose and chicken or duck livers. I don't have exact measures to offer, but go easy on the ginger.

> 2 or 3 wild goose livers
> butter
> sliced onion
> sliced mushrooms
> paprika
> ground ginger
> sugar
> sherry
> salt and pepper

Melt the butter in a skillet. Sauté the onion and mushrooms until the onion starts to brown. Take up and drain. Heat a little more butter if needed, then sauté the liver for a few minutes on each side. Add the onions and mushrooms back to the skillet. Sprinkle with paprika, sugar, ginger, salt, and pepper, stirring with a wooden spoon. Stir in a little sherry. Cover for a few minutes, then serve hot with rice, vegetables, and perhaps a baked apple.

Liver Pâté

This pâté can be made with duck or goose liver, or with a combination. In a pinch, a few chicken or rabbit livers can be added to fill out the measure.

> 2 pounds liver
> ⅔ cup goose, chicken, or pork fat, diced
> 3 chicken eggs
> 1½ cups whipping cream
> ½ cup flour
> ⅓ cup brandy
> 1 medium onion, chopped
> 1 tablespoon salt
> 3 teaspoons white pepper
> 1 teaspoon ground ginger
> 1 teaspoon freshly ground allspice

Preheat the oven to 325 degrees. Working in several batches, puree the liver, chicken eggs, brandy, and cream in an electric blender, adding a little of the onion, flour, and diced fat with each batch. When all the liver has been pureed, add the salt, ginger, white pepper, and allspice. Mix well. Turn the mixture into a well-greased ovenproof mold. Cover the top with heavy-duty aluminum foil. Bake in the center of the oven for 2 hours. Then turn off the oven and let the pâté sit in the oven for 20 to 30 minutes or so. Refrigerate until serving time. Serve on toast or crackers.

Whole Duck Pâté

Here's a pâté made with the whole duck, in case you don't have enough goose and duck livers.

      2 large wild ducks with giblets
      1 medium onion, quartered
      1 medium onion, minced
      ½ rib celery with tops, scraped and minced
      1 envelope gelatin
      10 juniper berries
      3 bay leaves
      1 tablespoon fresh thyme
      olive oil
      salt and pepper

Skin and disjoint the ducks, saving the giblets and bony parts. Set the liver aside. Place the other duck pieces and giblets into a pot. Cover with water. Add the quartered onion, bay leaves, and juniper berries; bring to a boil, cover, reduce heat, and simmer for 20 minutes. Add the liver and simmer for another 10 minutes, or until the meat is very tender. Drain the meat and strain the broth, discarding the bay leaves, juniper berries, and quartered onion. Bone the duck and chop all the meat. Heat a little olive oil in a skillet. Sauté the minced onion and minced celery for a few minutes. Put the chopped duck meat, gelatin, sautéed onion and celery, thyme, salt, pepper, and ½ cup of the reserved broth into a food processor. Blend, using the pulse mode. Add a little broth as needed to keep the mixture thin enough to flow. With the help of a large spoon, pour the mixture into a serving bowl. Cover and chill before serving as an appetizer, along with crackers.

Giblet Gravy

Here's one of my favorite ways to use giblets of ducks, geese, and other good birds.

The Giblets
liver
gizzard
heart
neck
backbone
head (optional)
feet (optional)
wing tips (optional)
3 bay leaves

Put all the innards and other parts, except for the liver, into a pot, and barely cover them with water. Add the bay leaves, and bring to a boil. Then cover, reduce the heat to very low, and simmer for 1 hour. Add the liver and simmer for another 20 minutes. Take out all the parts. Discard the bay leaves, but retain the pot liquid. When the giblets cool, pull the meat from the neck and backbone. Dice the gizzard and heart. Dice the liver, but keep it separate. If you have used the head, wing tips, and feet, save them for nibbling. The brain is very, very good, and the duck feet, something of a delicacy in China, make good conversation for those people who like to nibble on toes. Spit out the small bones.

The Gravy
giblets and stock
3 hard-boiled chicken eggs, sliced
2 tablespoons butter
2 tablespoons flour
1 medium onion, diced
salt and freshly ground pepper

Melt the butter in a skillet, and stir in the flour. Cook on very low heat for 10 minutes, stirring with a wooden spoon. Stir in the onions and cook for a few more minutes. Stir in the giblets, except for the liver, and add about 2 cups of the stock from the pot. Simmer until the gravy thickens a little. Add salt and pepper to taste. Add the liver and hard-boiled eggs, stirring carefully. Serve this gravy with sliced meat, or eat it over biscuits or toast. I prefer it over toast that has been well browned but unbuttered. Giblet gravy is also very good over rice.

Duck Giblet Soup

This old soup recipe is made with the giblets, neck, wings, rib cage, and feet from 4 mallard-size ducks, 1 large goose, 6 to 8 teal-size birds, or thereabouts. The exact measurements of giblets aren't too critical, and you can mix in some rabbit or chicken parts if needed.

giblets from 4 mallards or equivalent
½ cup butter
1 gallon boiling water
1 rib celery with tops, chopped
1 carrot, chopped
1 large onion, chopped
1 medium turnip, chopped
juice of 1 lemon
½ cup Madeira or port wine
4 bay leaves
2 sage leaves
parsley
hard-boiled chicken egg yolks
salt
cayenne pepper

Heat the butter in a large Dutch oven, and sauté the onion until it browns nicely. Add the chopped celery, carrot, turnip, and giblets. Cook for 10 minutes, stirring from time to time. Add the water, bony parts of fowl, bay leaves, sage leaves, and parsley. Cover tightly and simmer (do not boil) for 5 hours. Strain the broth. Mash one of the livers and stir it into the broth, discarding the rest of the giblets and bones. (If you are so inclined, feel free to nibble on the gizzards and other parts.) Stir in the Madeira or port. Season the soup to taste with salt, cayenne, and lemon juice. Steep for 10 minutes or longer, but keep hot. Place a hard-boiled chicken egg yolk in each bowl, pour in the soup, and serve hot.

Gizzard Purloo Cross Creek

A pilau always goes nicely as a side dish, especially when you don't have enough meat to feed everybody. I can make a complete meal of this dish if I've got some fresh tomatoes to slice and serve. When dressing the gizzards, be sure to slice them and empty the contents.

   10 or more duck or coot gizzards
   1 cup rice
   salt and red pepper flakes

Cut the gizzards in half, put the pieces into a pot, cover with water, and add the salt and red pepper flakes. Boil for an hour or two, or until the gizzards are very tender. Measure the broth and add 2½ cups back to the pot. (If necessary, add enough water to make 2½ cups of liquid.) Bring to a boil, add the rice, cover, reduce the heat, and simmer for 20 minutes. The pilau should be quite moist, but firm enough to serve as a side dish. If it is too soupy after simmering for 20 minutes, leave the cover off and simmer a little longer.

Note: This dish is made with coot gizzards down around Orange Lake, Florida, according to *Cross Creek Cookery,* by Marjorie Kinnan Rawlings.

Coot Gizzards with Black Beans

I fed this to my wife for lunch one day, and she said it was delicious. If you don't have enough coot gizzards to feed everybody, add a duck gizzard or two, or even chicken gizzards. In a pinch, sneak in a few mullet gizzards.

> 1½ pounds coot gizzards
> 2 cans white hominy (16-ounce size)
> ¾ pound smoked venison sausage
> 12 ounces dry black beans
> salt and flaked red pepper to taste
> water

Cut the dressed gizzards into fingers, then put them into a large pot or stove-top Dutch oven. Add the black beans, salt, and red pepper. Cover with quite a bit of water, remembering that the black beans will absorb water as they swell. Bring to a boil, then reduce the heat, cover, and simmer on very low for at least 1 hour, adding more water from time to time if needed. Cut the venison sausage into 1-inch pieces, add to the pot, and simmer for at least 30 minutes, or until the gizzards are tender and the black beans are done.

About 30 minutes before serving time, open the hominy, drain the juice from the cans, and heat the hominy in a little water in a separate boiler. Simmer for a few minutes, then drain. Spoon some hominy into individual serving bowls, then, using a slotted spoon, add some of the gizzard and black bean mixture to the center of the hominy, making an attractive dish. Add a little of the black juice from the pot to the center of the bowl, being careful not to discolor the white hominy. Serve for lunch with hot bread.

Goose Hearts Bashline

For this recipe—and idea—I am head over heels in debt to Sylvia Bashline, author of *The Bounty of the Earth Cookbook*, from which it has been adapted. For a long time I have eaten venison heart cooked and served on its own, but I cooked the hearts of waterfowl and small game along with the rest of the giblets. To get enough goose hearts to fool with, most of us will have to save them up in the freezer. It's best to freeze them in a block of ice. I use small plastic containers.

> goose hearts
> bay leaf
> onion slices
> vinegar
> salt and pepper
> water

Place the goose hearts in a pot with water to cover, along with salt, pepper, onion, and a bay leaf. Bring to a boil, then reduce the heat, cover, and simmer for 35 to 40 minutes, or until tender. Drain, cool, and thinly slice the hearts. Put them in a nonmetallic container and add enough water and vinegar, used half and half, to cover. Place the container in the refrigerator overnight. Drain, pat dry, and serve as appetizers or use for sandwiches.

Duck or Goose Jerky

As pointed out in my *Complete Fish & Game Cookbook*, duck or goose breast can be used to make jerky, and any good recipe for beef jerky will work. I like to keep mine simple. Skin the breast, trim off all fat, and slice the meat with the grain into pieces no thicker than ¼ inch. The slicing is easier if the fillets are partly frozen. Put the duck pieces into a nonmetallic container, cover with soy sauce, and add some crushed garlic. Marinate overnight in the refrigerator. Pat the duck pieces dry, then place them across the racks in your oven. Turn the oven to the lowest setting and leave them for 3 hours or longer, depending largely on the temperature of the oven. It's best to leave the oven door ajar, which will allow the moisture to escape and help keep the temperature low. Check the jerky from time to time, and take out of the oven when the pieces are dry.

If you live in a dry climate without many bugs, hang the jerky out on the clothesline during the day. Bring the meat into the house at night, then hang out again the next day. This slow drying process makes better jerky, in my opinion. Other people will want to speed the process up, even using a microwave oven to make jerky.

In any case, jerky that isn't eaten right away can be put into airtight jars and stored until needed. Refrigeration isn't necessary. After being prepared, the jerky can be gnawed, or soaked in water for use in soups and stews.

Duck Fingers

Serve this appetizer, perhaps with beer, while the gumbo simmers, or as a side dish to venison.

> duck breasts
> 1 cup clarified butter
> flour
> salt and pepper

Fillet the duck breasts, then cut the meat into ½-inch fingers. Sprinkle the fingers with salt and pepper, then shake them in a bag with a little flour. Heat the butter in a skillet. Over medium heat, sauté the fingers, a few at a time, until browned. Do not overcook. Serve hot.

Variations: Use garlic salt or lemon-pepper seasoning salt.

Dr. John's Sautéed Duck Appetizers

Here's a recipe from Dr. John Paul Forest of Annandale, Virginia, adapted from *Cookin' on the Wildside,* published by the Grand National Waterfowl Association.

> 4 duck breasts
> 1 cup chicken broth
> ½ cup soy sauce
> ½ cup dry red wine
> ⅓ cup honey
> ½ cup olive oil
> ½ cup butter
> 1 tablespoon cornstarch
> garlic
> salt and pepper

Mix the wine, soy sauce, and honey in a saucepan. Bring to a boil, then remove from the heat. Place the duck breasts in a nonmetallic container. Pour the wine mixture over them and marinate for several hours. Drain the duck breasts, retaining the marinade. Heat a little butter and olive oil in a skillet. Sear both sides of the breasts over high heat, then reduce the heat and sauté the breasts until they are medium rare. Add 1 cup of chicken stock to the reserved marinade along with the garlic, salt, and pepper. Bring to a light boil, and cook until the liquid is reduced by half. Add the cornstarch to a little water, then stir the paste slowly into the sauce until it thickens. Place the sauce in a small container in the center of a serving platter. Slice the duck breasts on a bias, and arrange the slices around the sauce bowl.

Giblet Stuffing

The measures in this recipe are calculated to provide ample stuffing for 1 large wild duck, using its own giblets. Increase as needed. The bread crumbs are from soft fresh bread, French or sourdough type.

>1 set duck giblets
>⅔ cup sourdough soft bread crumbs moistened
>	with milk
>brandy
>1 medium onion, chopped
>1 clove garlic, minced
>1 teaspoon minced fresh thyme
>salt and pepper

Simmer the duck giblets in a small pot until tender. Drain, mince, and mix with the bread crumbs, onion, garlic, thyme, salt, and pepper. Sprinkle with brandy. Refrigerate for 1 hour before using to stuff the duck for roasting.

Goose Neck Sausage

Always save the skin from goose and duck necks. Stuff these with your favorite sausage mix, tie the ends with cotton string, and use just as you would any other stuffed sausage. I like to use ground duck or goose with various spices. Remember that partly frozen meat is easier to grind. The bacon ends are scraps and are usually quite inexpensive. The red pepper is best when ground from dried pods with a mortar and pestle. If you use red pepper flakes, grind them down to reduce the size of the seeds, which, when mixed into the sausage, can give off too much heat in one bite and not enough in another. Be warned that ½ teaspoon of some of the very hot dried red peppers, such as habanero, will make the sausage too hot for most of us.

1½ pounds duck or goose meat
½ pound smoked bacon ends
1 teaspoon salt
½ teaspoon freshly ground red pepper
½ teaspoon sage

Cut the meat and bacon into small pieces. Spread these out, mixing them evenly, and sprinkle evenly with the salt, red pepper, and sage. Grind the meat, then stuff it into the goose neck, using a sausage stuffing tube or the neck of a plastic bottle or other suitable tapered container. Store the sausage in the refrigerator for a few days, or cook it immediately. I like to fry or braise it, covered, in an electric skillet. Good stuff.

If you don't have neck skins, use hog casings or simply shape the meat into patties.

ELEVEN

Marinades, Sauces, and Go-withs

MARINADES

Some marinades alter the flavor of meat and should be considered part of the recipe. Others are intended to tenderize the meat or take away a "gamy" flavor, or both.

Milk or Buttermilk

Ordinary milk is one of my favorite marinades for any game or waterfowl. It doesn't impart an overpowering flavor, but it seems to leave the meat with a clean odor and taste. Buttermilk will also work, and I like it especially with meat that is to be breaded and fried. In either case, use at least 2 or 3 cups of milk for each duck, and more for each goose. If you disjoint the bird, enough milk to cover it will be just right. If you use a whole bird or two in a Ziploc bag or other suitable container, turn it from time to time to make sure that the meat stays moist. Marinate in the refrigerator overnight or, better, for 24 hours.

Salt or Soda Marinade

The term *marinade* comes from the Latin *mare*, meaning "sea." It follows that salty seawater was the first marinade, or pickle. With salt, try 2 tablespoons per quart of water. With baking soda,

1 tablespoon. Of the two, I prefer soda, which leaves the meat with a clean taste, color, and odor. Cover the birds with the solution in a nonmetallic container. Refrigerate overnight, or for 24 hours.

Olive Oil and Red Wine

I like to use this marinade with ducks and geese that have been skinned, which tend to be dry when cooked.

> 1 cup olive oil
> ½ cup dry red wine
> 2 cloves garlic, crushed
> 10 peppercorns, crushed

Mix all the ingredients. Place the duck or duck pieces into a nonmetallic container or Ziploc bag. Pour in the marinade, turning the meat to coat all sides. Refrigerate overnight or, better, for 2 days.

Teriyaki Marinade

Use this marinade for duck meat that will be grilled, broiled, or stir-fried.

> 1 cup peanut oil
> ⅓ cup soy sauce
> ⅓ cup red wine vinegar
> ⅓ cup honey
> 2 tablespoons chopped green onions with tops
> 1 tablespoon grated fresh ginger root
> 2 cloves garlic, minced

Mix all the ingredients in a nonmetallic container. Add the meat (up to 3 or 4 pounds), toss to coat all sides, cover, and refrigerate for a day or longer.

Sesame Marinade

½ cup soy sauce
¼ cup Chinese sesame oil
juice of 2 large lemons
2 cloves garlic, crushed
1 tablespoon brown sugar
black pepper

Mix all the ingredients. Put the duck or duck parts into a large plastic Ziploc bag, pour in the marinade, and turn to coat all sides. Refrigerate overnight or at least 8 hours. Grill, broil, or stir-fry the duck meat.

Stuffing "Marinade"

A lot of cooks stuff a duck with the idea of altering the flavor, then throw the stuffing away. In other words, the stuffing acts like a sponge to take away strong flavor. Usually the stuffing is thrown out after roasting, but here's a recipe that works like a taste-improving marinade, used and discarded prior to cooking.

onion, sliced
lemon or lime, quartered
vinegar

Rub each duck inside and out with a cloth dampened with vinegar. Stuff each duck with sliced onion and quartered lemon or lime. Place in the refrigerator overnight. Discard the stuffing before cooking.

Dr. Frye's Coot Marinade

Dr. O. E. Frye, head of Florida's Fresh Water Fish and Game Commission, once said in an official news release, "It is indeed unfortunate that more sportsmen don't add a few coots to their waterfowl bag. The daily bag limit is a generous 15 per day [check the current bag limits] and the coot may be found throughout Florida. Bagging a coot is not much of a challenge to the average gunner and this, perhaps, may be one reason sportsmen tend to overlook the bird." The news release also made it clear that the secret to the coot recipe is in skinning the bird and removing all the fat before applying the marinade.

     1 quart good water
     1 cup white vinegar
     1 tablespoon salt

Mix the marinade and pour it over dressed coots or ducks in a nonmetallic container. Soak the coots overnight in the refrigerator or in a cool spot. The marinade should completely cover the coots, so mix more than one batch if needed.

Garlic Oil

I like to use garlic-flavored oil for sautéing and stir-frying, as well as for making toasted garlic bread. Although any good cooking oil can be used, I prefer olive or peanut oil. To make garlic oil, merely fill a jar with peeled garlic cloves, cover with oil, and set aside for a few weeks. A quicker method, which can give a distinctive burnt flavor, is to sauté some sliced garlic until it browns in some oil.

This oil can be used immediately for stir-frying or sautéing; as a baste for grilling or broiling; or, used sparsely, as a marinade.

A. D.'s Tabasco Oil

Fill a small jar with a mixture of red, green, and orange fresh whole Tabasco peppers. Cover with olive oil. After a week or so, use the oil sparingly to flavor stir-fry oils. Also use it very sparingly as a marinade.

SAUCES, CONDIMENTS, AND SPECIAL INGREDIENTS

The rich meat of ducks lends itself well to various sauces and table condiments. Many of these are sweet or sweet-and-sour.

Cranberry Sauce

This American favorite is often served with turkey, but it is also good with sliced duck or goose.

> 16 ounces fresh cranberries
> 1¼ cups sugar
> 1¼ cups water

Mix the water and sugar in a saucepan. Bring to a boil and add the cranberries. Bring to a new boil, then reduce the heat and simmer for 10 minutes, stirring every 2 minutes or so, or until the cranberries pop open. Let the mixture cool a bit, pour it into a serving dish or mold of suitable shape, and refrigerate until ready to serve.

Variation: American Indians and the early settlers in the Northeast used maple sugar to make cranberry sauce. Try it.

Cranberry-Orange Relish

This cranberry relish has an orange flavor, which is always good with duck and geese.

> 16 ounces fresh or fresh frozen cranberries
> 2 cups sugar
> ½ cup blanched almonds, slivered
> ½ cup fresh orange juice
> ½ cup water
> 2 teaspoons grated orange rind

Grate 2 teaspoons of orange peel from the outside, avoiding the bitter white pith. Mix all the ingredients except the almonds in a saucepan. Bring to a boil, then reduce the heat and simmer for 10 minutes, or until the cranberries pop open. Remove from the heat and skim the scum off the surface with a spoon. Stir in the almonds, pour the mixture into a serving container, and refrigerate until time to eat.

Wild Plum Sauce

> 1 quart wild plums
> water
> 3 tablespoons chopped cilantro
> 1 tablespoon freshly chopped basil
> ¼ teaspoon salt
> ¼ teaspoon Tabasco sauce

Put the plums into a saucepan, add enough water to almost cover them, and bring to a boil. Reduce the heat, cover, and simmer for about 20 minutes, or until the plums are soft. Take out the plums, reserving the liquid. Remove the pits from the plums, and put the meats into a blender or food processor. Add a little liquid from the saucepan. Zap the mixture and add a little more of the liquid. Continue until you have a thick sauce. Mix this sauce into the liquid in the saucepan. Stir in the cilantro, basil, salt, and Tabasco sauce. Serve with duck or goose.

Cumberland Sauce

The French tome *Larousse Gastronomique* says that this old British sauce is traditionally served with cold venison. The main ingredients are red currant jelly and oranges. I also insist on port, since the British love it so, but some cookbook authors leave this ingredient out. In any case, I find that Cumberland Sauce is better with roast duck than with venison. There must be a thousand variations. Here's mine:

> 1 cup red currant jelly
> 1 cup port
> 2 oranges
> 1 lemon
> 1 small white onion (golf-ball size), minced
> 1 tablespoon butter
> ½ teaspoon dry mustard
> salt
> 2 slices fresh ginger root
> cayenne
> hot water

Squeeze the juice from 1 orange. Zest the lemon, then squeeze the juice from it. Peel the second orange, cutting about a quarter of the peel into thin strips; blanch these in hot water, drain, and set aside. Slice the orange thinly and set aside. Melt the butter in a saucepan. Sauté the onion and ginger root for 3 or 4 minutes. Add the lemon juice, orange juice, lemon zest, and red currant jelly. Stir until the jelly melts. Add the port, mustard, blanched orange peel, orange slices, salt, and a little cayenne. (The cayenne should be used sparingly, adding a little at a time.) Simmer and stir for 20 minutes. Serve hot in a gravy boat, using the orange slices as a garnish.

Commercial Plum Sauce

Sometimes called duck sauce, this commercial sauce is widely available in oriental stores and supermarkets. It is a table sauce made from sour plums, apricots, chili, ginger, vinegar, and sugar. Thick, sweet, and pungent, plum sauce goes nicely with sliced duck or goose.

Hoisin Sauce

This Chinese sauce—thick, red brown, and sweet—goes nicely as a condiment with roast or steamed duck. It is made, for the most part, from soybeans, chili peppers, and garlic.

Oyster Sauce

This thick, brown sauce, available in Chinese markets, is made with brined oysters and soy sauce cooked down. Although rich in flavor, it is a good table condiment to serve with duck.

Apricot Sauce

Here's an easy sauce that goes nicely with roast, broiled, or grilled duck.

> ½ pound dried apricots
> 2 cups dark brown sugar
> ½ teaspoon ground allspice
> salt
> 5 cups water

Soak the apricots in the water for several hours, then simmer until they are soft. Puree the apricots, along with the water, in a blender or food processor. Put the mix into a saucepan, and stir in the brown sugar, allspice, and salt. Bring to a light boil, reduce the heat, and simmer for 5 minutes, stirring as you go. Serve hot over duck or goose.

Currant Sauce

This easy sauce goes with roast or grilled duck, or with sliced goose breast.

>1 jar red currant jelly (10-ounce size)
>¼ cup catsup
>¼ cup dark brown sugar
>¼ cup butter

Melt the butter in a small pan. Mix in the other ingredients. Stir until the mixture starts to boil, then remove from the heat. Serve warm.

Peach Sauce for Roast Duck

Here's an excellent duck sauce that I have adapted from *The Great Southern Wild Game Cookbook,* written by Sam Goolsby, president of Cedar Creek Hunting Lodge in Georgia—peach country. Goolsby called for fresh peaches, but I have found that fresh frozen fruit also works. He also listed "duck meat pan drippings" in his recipe. Presumably, this is taken from the roast duck on which the sauce is to be used. He didn't specify an amount, and I use 2 tablespoons. In his directions, Goolsby said to run the peaches and some other ingredients through a ricer or colander. A food mill will also work, as will a grater with a coarse mesh.

>2½ cups sliced peaches
>2 cups dry red wine
>4 duck livers
>2 tablespoons butter
>1 tablespoon grated orange peel
>2 tablespoons pan drippings
>pepper to taste

Run the peaches through a food mill. Grate the orange peel, avoiding the bitter inner white pith; it's easier to grate the peel from a whole orange, so that you have something to hold. Put the peaches, red wine, grated orange peel, and butter into a saucepan, bring to a boil, and reduce the heat to low. Run the livers through the food mill, then add to the saucepan, along with some pan drippings from the duck and a little pepper. Simmer for 20 minutes.

Applesauce

I love applesauce served with a big meal with rich meat. It's perfect with duck and dressing.

> 4 medium-to-large apples
> ½ cup sugar
> ¼ cup water
> 1 teaspoon ground cinnamon

Peel, core, and slice the apples. Put them into a pan, add the water, and boil until the apples soften. Mash with a potato masher. Stir in the sugar and cinnamon. Cook for a few more minutes, stirring as you go. Serve chilled.

Applesauce with Horseradish

Tart apples go nicely with the rich flavor of duck, and a little fresh horseradish root adds a piquant touch to keep you eating.

> 1 pound tart apples
> ¼ cup dry white wine
> 1 tablespoon grated horseradish root
> ¼ teaspoon lemon zest
> mayonnaise
> salt

Peel the apples and dice them. Put the diced apples into a pan with a tight lid, then add the wine, grated horseradish, lemon zest, and a little salt. Bring to heat, cover tightly, reduce the heat, and steam until the apples are soft. Then mash them thoroughly with a potato masher. Measure the apples and put them into a bowl. Add half as much mayonnaise, stir, chill, and serve with cooked duck.

Orange Sauce

Oranges figure nicely into many good duck recipes, making this sauce a natural accompaniment for roast or broiled duck. When you grate the orange rind, avoid the bitter white part.

>1 cup fresh orange juice
>1 cup brown sugar
>¼ cup Grand Marnier
>2 tablespoons grated orange rind
>1 tablespoon cornstarch
>5 or 6 drops Tabasco sauce

In a saucepan, mix the orange juice, brown sugar, Tabasco sauce, and cornstarch. Heat, stirring constantly, until the mixture thickens. Add the orange rind and Grand Marnier. Cook and stir for 1 minute. Serve warm over sliced duck.

Sherry Sauce

Here's an easy sauce for duck and venison. This sauce goes best with ducks or geese that have been cooked without the aid of herbs and spices, as in Duck Hewitt (chapter 1).

>½ cup sherry
>½ cup red currant jelly
>½ cup catsup

Melt the jelly in a small pan. Stir in the sherry and catsup. Serve warm with roast duck or goose.

Kumquat Marmalade

Technically, the thumb-size kumquat is not a citrus fruit, but it is citruslike and does make a good condiment for the rich dark meat of the wild duck and goose. For this recipe, cut the kumquats in half and remove the seeds. Then grind them in a food mill. Note that the peel is left on the kumquats, as it is the best part. The lemon is also seeded and ground in the same manner.

> 3 cups ground kumquat pulp
> 1 cup ground lemon pulp
> 4 cups water
> sugar

After grinding the fruit pulp, put it into a nonmetallic container and stir in the water. Let the mixture stand overnight. Then cook the mixture for 30 minutes, stirring as you go. Let it stand again overnight, preferably in the refrigerator. Measure the mixture in cups, put it into a saucepan, and bring to heat. Stir in an equal amount of sugar, cup by cup, and cook until the marmalade thickens. Have ready some small sterilized jars and lids. Pack the marmalade into jars and seal. Serve with roasted duck.

Cherry Sauce

This is a delicious sauce to serve with duck or goose.

> 1 can pitted cherries (16-ounce size)
> ½ cup dry red wine
> juice of ½ lemon
> 1 tablespoon cornstarch
> salt
> sugar

Drain the cherry juice into a skillet or saucepan. Stir in the wine, a little sugar, and cornstarch. Bring to a boil, reduce the heat a little, and cook until the mixture thickens, stirring as you go.

Stir in the lemon juice, cherries, and a little salt. Serve hot with sliced goose or duck breast.

Ginger Dipping Sauce

Here's a Vietnamese sauce that goes nicely with sliced roast duck.

½ cup soy sauce
¼ cup grated fresh ginger root
2 tablespoons sugar
2 tablespoons water
1 tablespoon white vinegar

Mix all the ingredients, and serve in individual bowls.

Lychee Sauce

If you like the Chinese lychee fruit as much as I do, this sauce might become one of your favorite condiments for serving with roast or steamed duck. Canned lychees can be found in most supermarkets or oriental food stores.

1 large can lychee fruit (16-ounce size)
1 cup chicken or duck broth
2 tablespoons plum jelly
1 tablespoon soy sauce
1 tablespoon honey
½ tablespoon brandy
paste of cornstarch mixed with water

Drain the lychees, pouring the juice from the can into a saucepan. Add the chicken broth, soy sauce, brandy, plum jelly, and honey. Bring to a light boil, reduce the heat, and simmer for 5 minutes. Slowly add some cornstarch paste, stirring constantly, until the sauce thickens. Stir in the lychee fruit. Serve warm over sliced duck.

Chilean Duck Sauce

This sauce is made with the aid of pan drippings from roast duck.

> juice of 1 orange
> ½ cup port wine
> ½ cup pan drippings from roast duck
> 1 tablespoon minced bacon
> 1 tablespoon minced onion
> paste of flour mixed with a little water
> salt and pepper

In a skillet, sauté the bacon and onion. Add the pan drippings, and stir in a little flour paste to thicken. Stir in the wine, orange juice, salt, and pepper. Simmer until the sauce is thick enough to suit you. Add a little more flour paste if necessary. Serve hot with roast duck.

Myron's 20 Gauge Wild Game Sauce

A commercial sauce brewed with soy sauce, red wine, water, brown sugar, unsulfured molasses, honey, fresh garlic, olive oil, balsamic vinegar, and a secret mix of spices, Myron's 20 Gauge works for a marinade, basting sauce, recipe ingredient, and table condiment. If you can't find it locally, write to Myron's Fine Foods, Orange, MA 01364, or call (508) 544-2820. Owner Myron Becker donates 5 percent of the purchase price to the protection and restoration of our natural resources.

The night before writing this entry, I used a little 20 Gauge in a stir-fry of thinly sliced duck breast, diced new potatoes, onion, and diced green tomato. It was delicious.

Chantellier's Rare Game Sauce

This good stuff goes nicely as a table condiment for waterfowl and venison, served either warmed or chilled. It is also an excellent baste for roast or grilled duck. It is made from tomatoes, vinegar, currant juice, corn syrup, sugar, pectin, citric acid, sodium citrate, dehydrated onions, spices, and garlic powder. Sound good? If you can't locate this one in local stores or mail-order outfits, write to Ol' Ruff Enterprises, Inc., Millbrook, NY 12545.

Coconut Milk

The coconut is now used in one way or another in the cuisine of most parts of the world, and coconut milk is a very important ingredient in many recipes in Africa and Indonesia.

Crack the coconut, remove the meat in chunks, and grate it into a suitable container. Pour over the grated meat an equal volume of hot water. Cool, then squeeze out the liquid and strain it. This is coconut milk. You can repeat the process several times, but the liquid will become weaker as you go. Thus, you can obtain weak or strong coconut milk. You can even obtain "cream" by letting the strong milk stand for several hours and then skimming off the rich top layer.

In order to make 1 cup of coconut milk, start with 1½ cups of grated meat and 1½ cups of hot water.

If you don't have a fresh coconut, you can substitute unsweetened desiccated grated coconut, available in packages or perhaps frozen. Also, you may be able to find canned or frozen coconut milk in supermarkets or specialty food stores or through mail-order. But be warned that the cream of coconut with piña colada recipes on the back is usually too sweet.

Clarified Butter

Butter has a wonderful flavor when used to pan-fry or sauté meats, but it tends to burn easily. This problem is due to "impurities" in the butter. To clarify the butter, heat a large chunk in a saucepan over low heat, but do not stir. Some of the impurities will rise to the top like foam; others will settle to the bottom. Carefully skim off the top, then pour the clarified butter into another container, leaving the sediment in the bottom of the pan. Clarified butter will heat to a much higher temperature without burning.

RICE AND STUFFING

Rice and wild rice almost always go well with duck, especially when the recipe provides gravy.

Long-Grain Rice

As a rule, its best to have fluffy rice, with each grain separate. There are several methods of cooking such rice. Here's mine.

> 1 cup long grain rice
> 2 cups water
> salt
> cooking oil

In a pot with a tight-fitting lid, heat the water to a boil, along with a little oil and salt. Add the rice, bring to a boil, reduce the heat, cover tightly, and cook on very low heat for exactly 20 minutes. Do not peek during the cooking time. Remove the pan from the heat, dip the bottom into a larger pan of cold water, and remove the top. Serve hot.

These measures will make enough rice for 2 to 4 people as served with duck or goose dishes. Double the recipe if more is needed.

Garlic Rice

Melt 4 tablespoons of butter in a skillet. Sauté 2 cloves of crushed garlic for 2 minutes. On low heat, stir in 1 cup of long-grain rice and stir continuously until the butter has been absorbed. Do not brown the rice. Quickly add 2 cups of chicken stock, along with a little salt and white pepper. Reduce the heat to very low and cook for 20 to 25 minutes, or until all the stock has been absorbed.

Rice with Mushrooms

This rich, tasty dish goes with duck or goose that has been cooked without stuffing or dressing.

> 1 cup long-grain rice
> 1 can onion soup (10½-ounce size)
> 1 soup can water
> ½ cup butter
> 4 ounces fresh mushrooms, chopped
> salt and pepper

Melt the butter in a large, deep skillet. (Most electric skillets are ideal.) Sauté the mushrooms for a few minutes. Add the rice and cook for 1 minute. Stir in the soup, water, salt, and pepper. Cook for about 30 minutes, adding more water if needed. Feeds 4 to 6 with a duck dinner.

Wild Rice

As I pointed out in my *Wild Turkey Cookbook* (on which this entry is based), several misconceptions about wild rice should be cleared up. Real rice is a grain; wild rice is the seed of an aquatic grass, *Zizania aquatica* and related species, such as *Zizania texana,* which grows in Texas. Wild rice grows widely in North America, not just in the upper Midwest, and it is harvested commercially in several states. Wild rice will grow in brackish as well as fresh water. It has been planted as food for ducks and other wildlife, in which case harvesting a little for the table won't hurt a thing; in fact, moderate harvesting may cause the wild rice to expand faster.

Surprisingly, there are several varieties of wild rice and several different grades; some "wild rice" is actually cultivated in irrigated ponds in California and harvested by machine. Some varieties have a short grain, others long, and some in between. Also, the size of the grain will vary from one individual grain to another, so grading is required for rice that is marketed.

No foolproof rules can be set forth here, but be warned that some kinds of wild rice require more water and much longer cooking time than others. In all cases, wild rice requires more water and a longer cooking time than ordinary rice. If you purchase commercially packaged wild rice, be sure to follow the directions on the box or bag. If you gather your own, you should proceed with what I call a ballpark recipe, as follows:

> 1 cup wild rice
> 3 cups water
> salt to taste

Rinse the wild rice in cold water and drain. Put it into a suitable pan, cover it with 3 cups of water, and add the salt. Bring to a quick boil. Reduce the heat, cover, and simmer for 30 minutes. Check the water level and test the rice. Add water as needed and cook until the grains are tender which may take up to 1 hour

One cup of wild rice when fully cooked will expand greatly, yielding from 3 to 4 cups.

Wild Rice Stuffing

Some stuffings are intended to be thrown out after the bird is roasted; others are "dressing," cooked separately and served with the bird. Here's a real stuffing, designed to be an important part of the meal. It's really best to serve a whole duck per person, so that they can spoon out the stuffing as they eat the duck.

> 1 cup cooked wild rice
> 4 ounces chopped mushrooms
> 1 medium onion, chopped
> 1 rib celery with tops, chopped
> 1 clove garlic, chopped
> 2 tablespoons chopped fresh parsley or cilantro
> 2 tablespoons butter
> 1 teaspoon dried rosemary
> salt and pepper

Melt the butter in a large skillet, then sauté the onion, celery, mushrooms, and garlic for a few minutes. Add the remaining ingredients, mix, and stuff the bird immediately before roasting.

Saffron Pilau

This recipe calls for duck stock, but you can substitute chicken stock or 1½ cups of hot water with 2 chicken bouillon cubes.

> 1 cup long-grain rice
> 1½ cups duck stock
> 2 tablespoons butter
> 1 medium tomato, chopped
> 1 medium onion, chopped
> 8 ounces fresh mushrooms, sliced
> salt and black pepper
> ¹⁄₁₆ teaspoon saffron

Rinse the rice well in cold water and drain. Using a little of the butter, sauté the onions and mushrooms for about 5 minutes in a skillet. Remove, drain, and set aside. Heat the stock. Measure out 1 tablespoon of stock and mix the saffron into it; set aside. Melt the rest of the butter in the skillet and fry the rice until it browns slightly. In a saucepan of suitable size, heat the duck stock to boiling, then stir in the saffron. Add the fried rice, tomato, onions, mushrooms, salt, and pepper. Bring to a boil, reduce the heat to low, cover, and simmer for 25 minutes. Don't peek. This technique works best with a thick saucepan that doesn't tend to burn the bottom.

148

Fried Rice

This recipe works best with cold precooked rice. Each grain of the rice should be separate, and the mass not sticky.

> 6 cups cooked rice, cold
> ⅓ cup olive oil
> 3 cloves minced garlic
> salt and freshly ground black pepper

Heat the oil in a large skillet. Sauté the garlic for 2 or 3 minutes. Add the rice and fry, stirring with a wooden spoon, until the rice is golden. Stir in some salt and pepper. Serve hot with duck. Feeds 4 to 6.

A Culinary Guide to Ducks and Geese

Most ducks and geese make very good eating if they are properly field dressed and expertly cooked. The exceptions are those that have been feeding heavily on fish, which often gives them a strong flavor. Naturally, some kinds of ducks and geese are better than others. Although there is no infallible guide to wild waterfowl, I believe the text below will hold generally true. At the same time, I want to point out that anyone who was brought up eating sea ducks will be more tolerant of the stronger flavor, which might put off landlubbers brought up eating grain-fed mallards. Moreover, the birds' eating of fish doesn't necessarily impart a strong flavor to the meat.

In the entries below, the common names of the fowl are listed in alphabetical order. Alternate and regional names are put in parentheses, and the scientific names are italicized.

The seasons and bag limits on ducks vary from year to year, and sometimes the season is closed or reduced for some birds. Be sure to check the current waterfowl laws before hunting.

WILD DUCKS

Black Duck (red leg, black mallard), *Anas rubripes*. This is primarily an eastern freshwater bird, wintering from the Great Lakes east to New England and south to Texas. Its diet is made up of one-third water creatures and two-thirds vegetation. It is usually good eating, depending partly on recent feeding patterns. The drake of this rather large wild duck weighs up to 3 pounds.

Bufflehead (butterball, dipper), *Bucephala albeola*. This small, fast-flying duck weighs about 1 pound. Its diet is essentially marine life, which can impart a strong flavor to the meat.

Canvasback (can), *Aythya valisineria*. This bird winters from British Columbia to Mexico and from Chesapeake Bay to Florida, Texas, and Central Mexico. The canvasback dives as deep as 30 feet to feed, and about 80 percent of its diet is vegetable matter. It is especially fond of wild celery, but it will concentrate at times on animal life. It usually makes excellent eating. This large wild duck weighs up to 3 pounds.

Eider, Common, *Somateria mollissima*. There are several kinds of common eiders, but all are large northern sea ducks. They sometimes weigh up to 5 pounds. They tend to be a little strong tasting and are usually skinned before cooking. Similar species include the **king eider** (*Somateria spectabilis*), **spectacled eider** (*Somateria fischeri*), and **Steller's eider** (*Polysticta stelleri*).

Gadwall (gray duck, gray mallard), *Anas strepera*. This bird winters all along the Pacific and Gulf coasts and up the Atlantic coast to New Jersey. Mexico, however, is its favorite wintering ground. The gadwall, which eats mostly pond weeds and other vegetation, is usually excellent table fare. It weighs about 2 pounds.

Goldeneye (whistler), *Bucephala clangula americana*. Often heard before it is seen, the goldeneye feeds mostly on marine life and sometimes has a strong flavor. It weighs up to 3 pounds.

Mallard (greenhead for drake; gray duck for hen), *Anas platyrhynchos platyrhynchos*. This popular duck ranges throughout North America, from Alaska to Mexico. It is usually very good eating, especially when it has been feeding extensively on fields of corn, rice, or other grain. The adult drake weighs 2½ to 3 pounds.

Merganser, Common (American merganser, goosander, sawbill, fish duck), *Mergus merganser americanus*. This large sea duck, which sometimes weighs over 3½ pounds, is a fish eater and usually has a strong flavor. It should be skinned. Smaller, related species include the **hooded merganser** (*Lophodytes cucullatus*), and **red-breasted merganser** (*Mergus serrator*).

Mottled Duck (black duck, summer duck), *Anas fulvigula maculosa.* This species is usually found along the Gulf of Mexico, ranging from Mississippi to Veracruz, Mexico. Weighing up to 3 pounds or a little better, this bird is about 70 percent vegetarian, often found in rice fields. It usually makes good eating. A similar nonmigratory bird, the **Florida Duck** (*Anas fulvigula fulvigula*), lives mostly in Florida, as the name implies.

Oldsquaw (long-tailed duck, sea pintail, cockertail), *Clangula hyemalis.* This sea duck is found in the arctic and subarctic regions. A fish eater, it should be skinned, marinated, and stewed. The male weighs 2 to 2¼ pounds, the female a little less.

Pintail (sprig, sprigtail, spike, spike tail), *Anas acuta acuta.* This bird winters over the lower two-thirds of the United States, throughout Mexico and Central America, and into South America. Because it feeds mostly on wild rice, pondweed, and cultivated grains, its flesh is usually toothsome. The drake weighs a little over 2 pounds.

Redhead (pochard), *Aythya americana.* Wintering from Washington to Mexico and New Jersey to North Carolina, the redhead can make very good eating if taken inland, where it prefers a diet of wild celery, bulrush, and other vegetation. Along the coast, the redhead is more likely to feed more heavily on animal matter, in which case skinning and marinating may be in order. This bird weighs about 2½ pounds.

Scaup, Greater (bluebill, broadbill), *Aythya marila mariloides.* This far-ranging duck can be found from Scotland to arctic Asia to North America. In this country, it winters from Maine to Florida and Alaska to Southern California. Although it will take to fresh water, it prefers salt water. It is primarily a meat eater, feeding on fish and shellfish, although it also eats seeds, roots, and leaves. Because of its diet, it is not considered prime table fare, and for best results it should be skinned, marinated, and stewed. This bird weighs about 2 pounds in the feather.

Scaup, Lesser (bluebill), *Aythya affinis.* This duck is very similar to the greater scaup, although it is a little smaller. From a culinary viewpoint, however, the lesser scaup is better, because it feeds more heavily on vegetation. It prefers fresh water to salt.

Scoter, Black (American scoter, coot, clack coot, sea coot, black duck), *Melanitta nigra americana.* This sea duck can have a strong flavor and is usually skinned prior to cooking. It averages about 2½ pounds. Similar species include the **surf scoter** *(Melanitta perspicillata)* and the **white-winged scoter** *(Melanitta fusca deglandi).*

Shoveler, Northern (shoveler, spoonbill, spoony), *Anas clypeata.* This species can be found over most of North and South America, as well as Hawaii. It feeds in mud, using its shovel-shaped bill to sift out insects, small fish, tadpoles, and such. Because of its diet, it is usually comparatively poor table fare. If you eat the shoveler, it's best to skin, marinate, and stew it. The drake of this species weighs up to 1½ pounds.

Teal, Blue-Winged (blue-wing, summer teal, white-faced teal), *Anas discors.* This small duck can be found throughout most of Canada and the lower forty-eight states. The blue-wing usually makes excellent eating with about 70 percent of its diet vegetable matter, but it will at times feed primarily on animal life. The male of this species weighs almost a pound in feathers, and the female is even smaller.

Teal, Cinnamon (red teal, red-breasted teal), *Anas cyanoptera septentrionulium.* A little smaller than the blue-winged teal, this duck feeds primarily on vegetation and makes excellent eating.

Teal, Green-Winged (green-wing, common teal), *Anas crecca carolinensis.* The green-winged teal, which winters over most of the lower forty-eight states, is even smaller than the blue-wing. Strictly a freshwater bird, the green-wing usually eats vegetable matter and almost always makes excellent eating.

Wigeon, American, (baldpate, gray duck), *Anas americana.* This bird winters along the Atlantic, Pacific, and Gulf coasts, on into Mexico. The wigeon, which prefers a diet of wild celery and wild rice, makes excellent table fare. The drake weighs about 2 pounds, sometimes a little more.

Wood Duck (woodie, summer duck, acorn duck, swamp duck, squealer), *Aix sponsa.* Almost extinct a few years ago, the woodie is now one of the most plentiful ducks in the eastern part of the United States. It nests in hollow trees—in the south as well as the north—and in man-made wood duck houses. It feeds extensively on acorns, seeds, nuts, wild rice, and such, making it an excellent bird for the table. The drake weighs up to 1½ pounds.

WILD GEESE

The wild goose makes excellent table fare, provided that it is not cooked too long. The large Canada can be used in many recipes that call for domestic goose, and both the snow goose and the white-fronted goose can be used in recipes that call for a Long Island duckling. The wild birds are not quite as fatty, which is a plus in my opinion, and the flavor is usually more adventuresome.

Atlantic Brant (sea goose, white-bellied brant), *Branta bernicla hrota.* In flight, this small goose of the Atlantic coast looks like a duck. The male weighs only 3½ pounds in the feathers.

Black Brant (Pacific brant), *Branta bernicla nigricans.* This small goose of the Pacific coast is similar to the Atlantic brant, with the male weighing in at 3¼ pounds in the feathers.

Canada Goose (honker, Canada), *Branta canadensis canadensis.* This bird feeds extensively in fields and grasslands, grazing on various grasses, seeds, and cultivated crops, and thus it makes excellent eating. These birds can live as long as twenty years, and the older ones are on the tough side. It can weigh up to 8¾ pounds in the feathers.

There are several subspecies of Canadas in North America. The largest, the **giant Canada** *(Branta canadensis maxima),* can weigh up to 12½ pounds in the feathers. The **cackling Canada** *(Branta canadensis minima),* is the smallest, with the male weighing 3½ pounds and the female 2¾ pounds.

Snow Goose, Greater (wavie, brant), *Chen caerulescens atlantica.* The greater snow goose, primarily an eastern bird, winters along the Atlantic coast from Maryland to South Carolina. The lesser snow goose winters from southern British Columbia down the West coast, and over to Texas and Florida. Although the meat is not quite as good as that of the Canada goose, the snow goose is still good table fare. The male snow goose weighs up to 7 pounds in the feathers, about the same size as a Long Island duckling, and it can be cooked in many of the same recipes.

Snow Goose, Lesser (blue goose, wavie, brant), *Chen caerulescens caerulescens.* This goose is a little smaller than the greater snow goose, with the male weighing in at about 6 pounds.

White-Fronted Goose (specklebelly, specklebelly brant, speck, laughing goose), *Anser albifrons frontalis.* In North America, the white-fronted goose winters from southern British Columbia south to the Gulf coast and Mexico. This bird is fond of grains and vegetation, making it excellent table fare. The male averages about 5½ pounds in the leathers, sometimes reaching better than 6 pounds.

COOTS

Although some of the saltwater ducks may be nicknamed coots, the real ones have pointed bills and their feet aren't webbed, putting them in the rail family. They swim in open water, seeming to nod their heads as they go, and can often be bagged on a duck hunt. They prefer shallow water, either fresh or brackish, over mud bottoms. When they are flushed, they seem to run on the water, splashing their wings, and getting airborne with some difficulty. Several species live in South America, and several more in Africa and from the British Isles across Eurasia to Japan. The United States, however, has only one species, called the **common coot.** It weighs about a pound or a little better in the feathers. It should be skinned before being cooked. It is usually stewed.

The coot is quite plentiful in some areas, and most states have generous bag limits. It is my hope that the recipes in this book will encourage more hunters to make better use of the coot.

APPENDIX B

Ten Steps to Better Ducks and Geese

As stated in the introduction to this book, the essential steps to toothsome ducks and geese, as well as to fish and game in general, do not begin in the kitchen. They start with the hunter.

1. Know your birds. Learn to recognize the various species before hunting waterfowl, not only to comply with the legal hunting seasons and bag limits, but also for culinary purposes. Ducks that have been feeding heavily on fish are edible but may require special handling and cooking.

Old birds are not quite as tender as young ones. Although most ducks are tender enough for easy eating, provided they are not dried out during cooking, geese can grow quite old, living twenty to twenty-five years. The size of the bird is not always a reliable indicator, but a large bird should be considered tough if you've got company coming for dinner.

2. Cool the meat quickly. Most people who write about cooking game stress prompt field dressing. I agree that it can be very, very important, especially in warm weather. The real purpose of field dressing, however, is not necessarily to remove the innards as such. The idea is to remove the body heat, and the innards contain a good deal of it. The opening made during field dressing also permits a little air circulation. Thus, field dressing enables the meat to cool down quicker. Removing this heat is especially important when dealing with ducks and geese, because their feathers are such good insulation. The larger the bird and the warmer the temperature in the duck blind (or wherever the birds are kept), the more important prompt field dressing becomes. It's almost always a mistake to keep undrawn birds in the game compartment of a hunting jacket for any length of time. Of course, field dressing also permits you to cool the liver, gizzard, and heart quickly, if you want these delicacies. If the birds are badly shot up, field dressing may also prevent the innards (especially juice from the gallbladder) from giving the meat a bad flavor.

Duck hunting is often associated with cold weather, but this is not always the case. As I write these words, sitting in my cabin on Florida's Dead Lakes, it's shirtsleeve weather—yet the season is open for wood ducks and teal. In weather like this, it's best to either draw the birds promptly or put them on ice—or both. Plucking, discussed next, will also help cool the birds.

3. Pluck your birds. In almost all cases, it's better to pluck the birds than to skin them. Granted, plucking takes more time, but the end results are worth it. The skin holds in the moisture during cooking. Because duck and goose meat tend to be on the dry side, this is very important when cooking the birds with a dry heat method, such as baking (roasting), broiling, and grilling. Plucked ducks also keep better when frozen, as the skin keeps the air away from the meat.

It's usually easier to pluck the bird at the blind while the meat is warm. But some folks don't see it that way. Many hunters will nod agreement—but still don't do so.

There are several ways to pluck birds, such as dipping them in paraffin or wetting them in a bucket. Some people even use mechanical pickers or hire someone to do the plucking. I confess that I prefer the old-fashioned way—that is, simply pulling the feathers out with the fingers. Pull in the direction in which the feathers are growing.

In any case, the plucking job is not complete until all the pinfeathers have been pulled out. Many people pluck the birds quickly in the duck blind or afield, saving the pinfeathers for the kitchen. Tweezers or small needlenose pliers help. Many people singe the bird, sometimes using burning newspapers or even a blowtorch. I allow this, up to a point. But it's best to remove the larger pinfeathers before singeing. Remember that too much singeing can give the skin a bad flavor.

If you plan to hang or age the birds (step 4), it's best to leave the feathers intact until this process is completed.

Those people who skin ducks usually save only the breast, but the whole bird can be skinned, thereby saving the legs and thighs as well as the bony parts. I recommend saving the whole bird, especially with geese, which have some large, good thighs. In any case, skinned birds are usually prepared by a wet cooking method, and especially for making soups, stews, and casseroles. There can be exceptions, such as wrapping the meat with bacon before grilling, or perhaps broiling thin breast fillets close to the heat for a short period of time.

Many people remove the skin and all traces of fat from coots and fish-eating ducks because they believe that the "wild" taste resides there. I endorse the practice, but remember that this taste is not, to some people, as foul as commonly believed. Some people like it; others don't. Generally, those people who live in coastal areas and have a heritage of hunting and eating sea ducks are more likely to accept them as prime table fare.

4. Age the meat. As with venison and prime beef, ducks and geese are at their best when aged for a few days in a cool place before being cooked. How long? There is no set rule, but two days on the porch (or perhaps longer in cold weather) or five days in the refrigerator will be about right for ducks and geese. Any cool place will do, provided that neighborhood cats or varmints can't get at the birds. I usually put mine in the refrigerator, on the bottom rack and back toward the rear so that maybe my wife won't see 'em. The birds should not be frozen at night and thawed during the day, as might happen if they are left on the porch in cold weather.

It's best to age the birds with the feathers still on them, except perhaps when they are to be frozen. Some people may still practice the old European custom of hanging the birds without drawing them. Some practitioners hang them by the neck until they fall by their own weight, and others hang them by the feet. Birds hung until the point of putrefaction were said to be high—a desirable state according to some of the old French gourmets.

In any case, the average modern man (and almost all women) doesn't want his birds to be high and, in fact, errs in the other direction. I'll have to say that I have eaten perfectly good ducks and smaller birds without any aging at all, but, in general, a few days in the cooler will indeed improve the flavor and texture. I do, however, prefer to gut the birds, although I have to admit that I often freeze birds whole, as discussed in the next step. Freezing, I might add, can be considered a form of aging, and one that I endorse. It's best to freeze birds fresh instead of aging them and then freezing them.

5. Freeze and thaw properly. If you draw and pluck the birds before freezing, it's best to wrap them tightly in freezer paper or button, freeze them in a block of ice. Milk cartons work nicely for this purpose. Those in ice will usually keep much longer than those wrapped in paper. Skinned birds and breast fillets are best frozen in ice, although they can also be wrapped in freezer paper.

I confess that I sometimes freeze small birds whole—feathers, innards, and all—thereby delaying the dressing and plucking process. Further, I have kept such frozen birds for almost a year. The key here, I think, is having birds that were cooled down shortly after the kill and kept cool, preferably on ice, until frozen. (Small birds such as teal and wood ducks cool down much quicker than larger birds.) Another key is in having birds that have not been shot up badly. Usually, these whole birds should be wrapped in freezer paper, but I confess to putting them directly into the freezer with feathers exposed. It's best to space the birds well apart rather than in a pile until they are frozen.

Most experts recommend thawing meat out in the refrigerator, but this process takes a long time. I usually thaw my ducks in the sink. If I am pressed for time, I'll run warm water over them. If desperate, I'll even thaw them out in the microwave. But slow thawing in the refrigerator is almost universally recommended, and I endorse the practice.

One other note: Be sure to identify the birds when you freeze them in blocks of ice or in wrapping paper. I recommend using freezer tape and a special pen with ink that won't blur. In addition to the kind of bird and date, also jot down the condition of the bird, such as whether or not it is badly shot up.

6. Get out the shot. Everyone who eats birds and small game taken with a shotgun will chomp down on a shot from time to time. I don't see any way to avoid the experience, but the careful hunter can minimize it. Carefully look for shot holes when you dress the birds, then dig the shot out with a small knife or tweezers. That's about the best you can do.

7. Select recipes thoughtfully. If your guests are squeamish about wild meat, do not put a whole bird on the table—and certainly not one that is cooked rare. It's also best to cook the bird in a familiar way, such as country-frying the breast fillets of young, tender birds. Stews are always good, and a duck or goose gumbo, if properly prepared, will surely draw a request for seconds and might even persuade a casual squirrel hunter to slosh toward a duck blind before sunup.

When birds are badly shot up, never cook them whole. Instead, reduce the meat to chunks for stew or soup, or dice or grind it for a casserole.

If the birds have been eating fish, select a recipe that calls for skinning the bird, trimming off any fat, and using a marinade.

Whenever you suspect that you have an old bird (especially a Methuselah goose), it's best to stew it instead of roasting it.

8. Pay attention to details. Prepare and cook your birds carefully. Remember that a long, complicated recipe guarantees nothing. Often the simple recipes, cooked with tender loving care, make the best eating. Use good ingredients, such as freshly ground black pepper instead of boxed pepper and fresh herbs instead dried.

9. Practice good "tablemanship." Set a pretty table, paying attention to color and atmosphere as well as to the taste of the food. A whole goose or two in the center of the table, or a smaller bird on each plate, can add to the atmosphere if you are feeding hunters—but it can have the opposite effect on other guests. If you do serve whole birds, remember that carving duck or goose is different from carving chicken or turkey. For one thing, the leg joints are in a different position. It's best to practice carving in the kitchen before attempting it at the table. If you think that you or your guests might have a problem, disjoint the bird and fillet out the breasts; then put it back together for your guests.

A bird supper is special. Have plenty to eat. Remember also that a dry red wine is especially good with duck or goose.

10. Don't hunt at the table. If you are having guests, refrain from telling about how Carl, your retriever, chased a cripple into the next county. Your wife also might be tired of hearing the story.

APPENDIX C

Metric Conversion Tables

U.S. Standard measurements for cooking use ounces, pounds, pints, quarts, gallons, teaspoons, tablespoons, cups, and fractions thereof. The following tables enable those who use the metric system to easily convert the U.S. Standard measurements to metric.

Weights

U.S. Standard	Metric	U.S. Standard	Metric
.25 ounce	7.09 grams	11 ounces	312 grams
.50	14.17	12	340
.75	21.26	13	369
1	28.35	14	397
2	57	15	425
3	85	1 pound	454
4	113	2	907
5	142	2.2	1 kilogram
6	170	4.4	2
7	198	6.6	3
8	227	8.8	4
9	255	11.0	5
10	283		

Liquids

U.S. Standard	Metric	U.S. Standard	Metric
¹/₈ teaspoon	.61 milliliter	³/₈ cup	90 milliliters
¹/₄	1.23	¹/₂	120
¹/₂	2.50	²/₃	160
³/₄	3.68	³/₄	180
1	4.90	⁷/₈	210
2	10	1	240
1 tablespoon	15	2	480
2	30	3	720
¹/₄ cup	60	4	960
¹/₃	80	5	1200

To convert	multiply	by
Ounces to milliliters	the ounces	30
Teaspoons to milliliters	the teaspoons	5
Tablespoons to milliliters	the tablespoons	15
Cups to liters	the cups	.24
Pints to liters	the pints	.47
Quarts to liters	the quarts	.95
Gallons to liters	the gallons	3.8
Ounces to grams	the ounces	28.35
Pounds to kilograms	the pounds	.45
Inches to centimeters	the inches	2.54

To convert Fahrenheit to Celsius: Subtract 32, multiply by 5, divide by 9.

Index

A Book of Middle Eastern Food (Roden),
   57
A. D.'s duck pie, 94–95
A. D.'s duck soup, crock-pot-style,
   109–10
A. D.'s electric skillet duck, 31
A. D.'s kumquat duck with leftovers,
   71–72
A. D.'s rotisserie duck, 84–85
A. D.'s Tabasco oil, 134
A double-barreled duck recipe, 70–71
A General's Diary of Treasured Recipes
   (Dorn), 28
After the Hunt Cookbook, 95
Aging meat, 158–59
Ames, Francis H., 2
Angier, Bradford, 19
Angolan duck with grilled papaya, 80–81
Appetizers
   duck fingers, 126
   goose hearts Bashline, 125
   liver with bacon, 118
   liver pâté, 119
   sautéed duck, Dr. John's, 127
   whole duck pâté, 120
Applesauce, 139
   with horseradish, 139–40
Apricot sauce, 137
Azerbaidzhani goose, 40–41

Baking soda marinade, 130–31
Barnett, Harriet and James, 60
Barsness, John, 5
Bashline, Sylvia, 89, 125
Beard, James, 1
Becker, Myron, 70, 143
Big grill duck, Chinese-style, 83
Black beans, coot gizzards with, 124
The Bounty of the Earth Cookbook
   (Bashline), 89, 125
Brazilian duck, 56–57
Broiled coot breast, 90–91
Broiled duck halves, 88
Broiled teal, 88–89
Broiling, 87
*Bull Cook and Authentic Historical
   Recipes* (Herter), 5
Burger, duck, 51–52

Butter, clarified, 144
Buttermilk marinade, 130

Cabbage
   goose and, easy, 63–64
   red, roast wild duck with, 10
      Russian goose with, 13–14
Cacciatore garigliana, 60–61
Camp, Ray, 60
Camp fried duck, 48
Campfire duck, 79–80
Caspian Sea duck kabobs, 78–79
Casserole(s)
   duck, supreme, 95–96
   duck Normandy, 96
   easy duck breast, 97
   Mexican duck, 97–98
   Outer Banks, 99–100
   R. C.'s favorite, 100
Cassis, 39
   sauce, duck with, 39
Chantellier's rare game sauce, 143–44
Chef Alfred's roast wild goose, 24
Cherry sauce, 141–42
Chestnuts, wild goose with, 68
Chilean duck sauce, 143
Chinese duck soup, 114–15
Chinese-style Canada goose, 64–65
Chunky duck stew, 111
Clarified butter, 144
Clay pot duck, 7–9
Coconut milk, 36, 144
Complete Fish & Game Cookbook
   (Livingston), 18, 48, 109, 125
Concord Farms, 39
Cookin' on the Wild Side, 100
Cooking from the Caucasus (Uvezian), 40
Coot, 155
   Armagnac, 22
   breast, broiled, 90–91
   gizzards, with black beans, 124
      purloo Cross Creek, 123
   marinade, Dr. Frye's, 133
   stew, Judy Marsh's, 112–13
Cranberry
   orange relish, 135
   sauce, 134
Creole stewed duck, 72–73

Crock-pot ducks, 65
Crock-pot goose thighs, 66
Cross Creek Cookery (Rawlings), 123
Cumberland sauce, 136
Currant jelly
  in Cumberland sauce, 136
  sauce, 138
Curry, Indian, 36
Czarnina, 115–16

Daylilies, 61–62
  duck and, 61–63
Dr. Frye's coot marinade, 133
Dr. John's sautéed duck appetizers, 127
Dorn, Frank, 28
Dress 'Em Out (Smith), 85
Duck
  appetizers, Dr. John's sautéed, 127
  and bacon on a spit, 85
  Baltimore, wild, 9–10
  Barsness, 5
  big grill, Chinese-style, 83
  Brazilian, 56–57
  breast, casserole, easy, 97
    fricassee, 43
    kiwi, 50–51
    teriyaki, 77–78
  burger, 51–52
  in cacciatore garigliana, 60–61
  camp fried, 48
  campfire, 79–80
  casserole, Mexican, 97–98
    supreme, 95–96
  with cassis sauce, 39
  clay pot, 7–9
  with corn, Rumanian roast, 15
  creole stewed, 72–73
  crock-pot, 65
  in Czarnina, 115–16
  and daylilies, 61–63
  a double-barreled recipe, 70–71
  easy camp, 45
  easy Chinese, 11
  easy grilled, 76
  electric skillet, A. D.'s, 31
  in faisinjan, 32
  fingers, 126
  fried sea, Fred's, 54
  Genghis Khan, 5–7
  giblets, soup, 122–23
    stuffing, 128
  gizzards, purloo Cross Creek, 123
  golden fried, 52–53
  good ol' boy, 76–77
  with gravy, wild, 49
  grill-ahead, 79
  with grilled papaya, Angolan, 80–81
  guava, the General's, 29–30
  Gulf City, 61
  gumbo, easy, 101–2
  halves, broiled, 88
  honey, 18–19
  jerky, 125–26
  John Hewitt, 2–4
  kabobs, Caspian Sea, 78–79

kumquat, with leftovers, A. D.'s, 71–72
liver, with bacon, 118
  pâté, 119
  with mushrooms, wild, 35
neck sausage, 128–29
New England braised wild, 63
of '94, 33–34
Normandy, 96
old, Bradford Angier, 19
old New England roast wild, 21
in Outer Banks casserole, 99–100
pâté, whole, 120
in pato con arroz, 46–47
Picayune canvasbacks, 17–18
pie, A. D.'s, 94–95
  easy, 93–94
  teal, 92–93
pressure-cooked, 66–67
pseudonym medium-rare, 2
in a pot, 1
with red cabbage, roast wild, 10
with rice, stewed, 107
rotisserie, A. D.'s, 84–85
with rum, roast, 7
salad, 74
sauce, Chilean, 143
sea, Elizabeth's favorite, 42
skillet, according to Dr. Carver, 45–46
smoked, Chinese-style, 81–82
  easy, 84
soup, Chinese, 114–15
  crock-pot-style, A. D.'s, 109–10
species, 150–54
steamed, Chinese-style, 69–70
stew, chunky, 111
  with easy dumplings, old, 107–8
stir-fried, 50
stock, 116
teal, broiled, 88–89
  jambalaya, 37–38
  and mushroom stew, 112
  pie, 92–93
  and venison sausage gumbo, 105–6
Turkish two-pot, 57–58
and turnips, Justin Wilson's, 58–59
  with turnips, stewed, 73
twice-baked, 12–13
in vathoo kari, 36–37
and vegetable soup, easy, 108–9
and venison sausage filé gumbo, 103–4
Ducks Unlimited Cookbook, 45
Dumplings, easy, old duck stew with,
  107–8
Dyer, Carole, 112

Easy camp duck, 45
Easy Chinese duck, 11
Easy duck breast casserole, 97
Easy duck gumbo, 101–2
Easy duck pie, 93–94
Easy duck and vegetable soup, 108–9
Easy goose and cabbage, 63–64
Easy goose gumbo, 101–2
Easy grilled duck, 76

Easy smoked duck, 84
Elizabeth's favorite sea duck, 42

Faisinjan, 32
Fenugreek, 36
Field dressing, 156–57
Filé, 101
The Forgotten Art of Flower Cookery
(Smith), 62
Fred's fried sea duck, 54
Freezing and thawing, 159
Fried rice, 149
Fried snow goose, 53–54
Frye, O. E., 133

Game Cookery (Sturdivant), 2
Game and Fish Cookbook (Barnett), 60
Garlic
oil, 133
rice, 145
The General's guava duck, 29–30
Giblets, 117
gravy, 121–22
stuffing, 128
see also individual names
Gin, Maggie, 69
Ginger dipping sauce, 142
Gizzards
with black beans, coot, 124
purloo Cross Creek, 123
Golden fried duck, 52–53
Golden fried goose, 53
Good ol' boy ducks, 76–77
Goolsby, Sam, 18, 138
Goose
Azerbaidzhani, 40–41
in a bag, roast, 23
breast, fricassee, 43
sautéed, 44
Sylvia's wild, 89–90
and cabbage, easy, 63–64
with chestnuts, wild, 68
Chinese-style Canada, 64–65
clay pot, 7–9
in Czarnina, 115–16
fried snow, 53–54
giblet soup, 122–23
golden fried, 53
gumbo, easy, 101–2
with oysters, 104–5
hearts Bashline, 125
jerky, 125–26
liver, with bacon, 118
pâté, 119
sautéed, 118–19
Native American stuffed, 20–21
neck sausage, 128–29
with oysters, roast, 25–26
in R. C.'s favorite, 100
with red cabbage, Russian, 13–14
with rice stuffing, 16
roast, Chef Alfred's, 24
salad (variation), 74
with sauerkraut, roast, 14
smoked, 85–86

species, 154–55
stock, 116
thighs, crock-pot, 66
Gormley, R. C., 100
Gourmet Cooking for Free (Angier), 19
Gourmet and Gourman (Wilson), 58
Gravy, giblet, 121–22
*The Great Southern Wild Game Cook-
book* (Goolsby), 18, 138
Grill-ahead duck, 79
Grilling, 75–76
Gulf City Cook Book, 61
Gulf City duck, 61
Gumbo(s), 101
duck, easy, 101–2
and venison sausage filé, 103–4
goose, easy, 101–2
with oysters, 104–5
teal and venison sausage, 105–6

Havana, Florida, 27–28
Hearts, goose, Bashline, 125
Herter, George Leonard, 5
Hewitt, John, 2–4
Hickoff, Steve, 42
Hoisin sauce, 137
Honey duck, 18–19
Horseradish, applesauce with, 139–40

Jambalaya, 37
teal, 37–38
Jerky, duck or goose, 125–26
Judy Marsh's coot stew, 112–13
Justin Wilson's duck and turnips, 58–59

Kavasch, Barrie, 20
Kircheis, Fred, 54
Kiwi, 33, 34
duck breast, 50–51
Kumquat, 71
duck with leftovers, A. D.'s, 71–72
marmalade, 141

Larousse Gastronomique, 136
Liver
with bacon, 118
pâté, 119
sautéed goose, 118–19
Livingston, Helen N., 27
Long-grain rice, 145
Lychee sauce, 142

MacDonald, Duncan, 21
The Maine Way (Marsh and Dyer), 54, 112
Marinade(s), 130
coot, Dr. Frye's, 133
garlic oil, 133
milk or buttermilk, 130
olive oil and red wine, 131
salt or baking soda, 130–31
sesame, 132
stuffing, 128
Tabasco oil, A. D.'s, 134
teriyaki, 131
Marmalade, kumquat, 141

Marsh, Judy, 112
Metaxa, John, 5
Metric conversion tables, 162–63
Mexican duck casserole, 97–98
Milk marinade, 130
Mushrooms
  Chinese black, 114
  rice with, 146
  and teal stew, 112
  wild duck with, 35
Myron's Fine Foods, 143
Myron's 20 gauge wild game sauce, 143

Native American stuffed goose, 20–21
Native Harvests (Kavasch), 20
New England braised wild duck, 63

*The Official Louisiana Seafood & Wild
  Game Cookbook*, 12
Oil
  garlic, 133
  olive, and red wine marinade, 131
  Tabasco, A. D.'s, 134
Okra, 101
Ol' Ruff Enterprises, Inc., 144
The Old Country Cookbook (Oleksy), 115
Old duck Bradford Angier, 19
Old duck stew with easy dumplings, 107–8
Old New England roast wild duck, 21
Old-Time New England Cookbook
  (MacDonald and Sagenorph), 21
Oleksy, Walter, 115
Olive oil and red wine marinade, 131
Onion and orange salad, 30
Orange(s)
  cranberry relish, 135
  in Cumberland sauce, 136
  and onion salad, 30
  sauce, 140
Our Best Recipes (Southern Living), 24
Outer Banks casserole, 99–100
Oyster(s):
  goose gumbo with, 104–5
  roast geese with, 25–26
  sauce, 137
  stuffing, 25

Papaya, grilled, 81
  Angolan duck with, 80–81
Pâté
  liver, 119
  whole duck, 120
Pato con arroz, 46–47
Peach sauce for roast duck, 138–39
Picayune canvasbacks, 17–18
Picayune Creole Cook Book, 17, 72
Pie(s)
  A. D.'s duck, 94–95
  easy duck, 93–94
  teal, 92–93
Pilaf, rice, 40–41
Plucking, 157–58
Plum sauce
  commercial, 137
  wild, 135

Pomegranate, 32
  syrup, 78
Pots, 55–56
  clay, 7–8
  crock, 55
  Dutch oven, 55
  pressure cooker, 55
Pre-Hispanic Cooking, 47
Pressure-cooked duck, 66–67
Pseudonym medium-rare duck, 2

Rare roast duck, 1
Rawlings, Marjorie Kinnan, 123
R. C.'s favorite, 100
Red wine and olive oil marinade, 131
Regional Cooking of China (Gin), 69
Relish, cranberry-orange, 135
Rhubarb, 5–6
Rice
  fried, 140
  garlic, 145
  long-grain, 145
  with mushrooms, 146
  pilaf, 40–41
  in saffron pilau, 148
  stuffing, goose with, 16
  see also Wild rice
Roast duck with rum, 7
Roast geese with oysters, 25–26
Roast goose in a bag, 23
Roast goose with sauerkraut, 14
Roast wild duck with red cabbage, 10
Roden, Claudia, 57
Rumanian roast duck with corn, 15
Russian goose with red cabbage, 13–14

Saffron pilau, 148
Sagenorph, Robb, 21
Salad(s)
  duck, 74
  goose (variation), 74
  orange and onion, 30
Salt marinade, 130–31
Sauce(s)
  apricot, 137
  Chantellier's rare game, 143–44
  cherry, 141–42
  Chilean duck, 143
  cranberry, 134
  Cumberland, 136
  currant, 138
  ginger dipping, 142
  hoisin, 137
  lychee, 142
  Myron's 20 gauge wild game, 143
  orange, 140
  oyster, 137
  peach, for roast duck, 138–39
  plum, commercial, 137
    wild, 135
  sherry, 140
Sauerkraut, roast goose with, 14
Sausage(s)
  goose neck, 128–29

venison, and duck filé gumbo, 103–4
  and teal gumbo, 105–6
Sautéed goose breast, 44
Sautéed goose livers, 118–19
Sesame marinade, 132
Sherry sauce, 140
Skillet duck according to Dr. Carver, 45–46
Skinning, 158
Smith, James A., 85
Smith, John A., 22
Smith, Leona Woodring, 62
Smoked duck, Chinese-style, 81–82
Smoked goose, 85–86
Smoking, 75–76
Soup(s), 101
  Chinese duck, 114–15
  Czarnina, 115–16
  duck, crock-pot-style, A. D.'s, 109–10
  duck giblet, 122–23
  duck and vegetable, easy, 108–9
  stock, duck, 116
    goose, 116
Southern Living magazine, 24
Spicebush, 20
Steamed duck, Chinese-style, 69–70
Stew(s)
  chunky duck, 111
  coot, Judy Marsh's, 112–13
  duck with rice, 107
  old duck, with easy dumplings, 107–8
  teal and mushroom, 112
  see also Gumbos
Stewed duck with rice, 107
Stewed duck with turnips, 73
Stir-fried duck, 50
Stocks. *See* Soups
Stuffing(s)
  giblet, 128
  marinade, 132
  oyster, 25

rice, goose with, 16
wild rice, 147–48
Sturdivant, E. N. and Edith, 2
Sylvia's wild goose breast, 89–90

Tabasco oil, 134
Tanner, Sherry, 95
Teal
  broiled, 88–89
  jambalaya, 37–38
  and mushroom stew, 112
  pie, 92–93
  and venison sausage gumbo, 105–6
Teriyaki marinade, 131
Trueblood, Ted, 2
Turkish two-pot duck, 57–58
Turnips, 73
  duck and, Justin Wilson's, 58–59
  stewed duck with, 73
Twice-baked ducks, 12–13

Uvezian, Sonia, 40

Vathoo kari, 36–37
Venison sausage
  and duck filé gumbo, 103–4
  and teal gumbo, 105–6

Whole duck pâté, 120
Wild duck Baltimore, 9–10
Wild duck with gravy, 49
Wild duck with mushrooms, 35
Wild Game Cookbook (Smith), 22
Wild goose with chestnuts, 68
Wild plum sauce, 135
Wild rice, 146–47
  stuffing, 147–48
Wild Turkey Cookbook (Livingston), 146
Wilson, Justin, 58
The World Atlas of Food, 114